de Lacy Chronicles

A history of the de Lacy family

Roy A Lacy

Copyright © 2016 Roy A Lacy

Roy A Lacy is hereby identified as the sole author of the entire works herein and reserves all of his rights to be identified as such and does not give his permission for any of material to be used. With the exception of dates, names and places which belong to history. However, up to 200 words may be used for educational or promotional use providing the title de Lacy Chronicles, and author Roy A Lacy are included.

Cover Picture

The Great Seal of Henry de Lacy

3rd Earl of Lincoln, 8th Baron of Pontefract,
9th Baron of Halton, 9th Lord of Bowland,
1st Lord of Denbigh
King's confidant

This book is

dedicated to my grandson

Louis Audain

Without his ever-present curiosity and enthusiasm this book would never have been written

CONTENTS

Intoduction 07

The Origins of the de Lacy Family 11

PONTEFRACT AND POLITICS 17

Ilbert de Lacy 18

Robert de Lacy 23

Ilbert de Lacy (II) 26

Henry de Lacy 29

Robert de Lacy (II) 34

Albreda de Lisours (nee de Lacy) 36

Roger de Lacy 37

John de Lacy Earl of Lincoln 44

Edmund de Lacy 50

Henry de Lacy 3rd Earl of Lincoln 53

THE MARSHER WAR LORDS **70**

Walter de Lacy   72

Roger de Lacy   74

Hugh de Lacy   80

Walter de Lacy (II)   81

Gilbert de Lacy   81

Hugh de Lacy   87

PASSAGE TO IRELAND **90**

Hugh de Lacy (cont)   94

Walter de Lacy   141

Hugh de Lacy (II) Earl of Ulster 101

William Gorm de Lacy   101

THE GREY YEARS **117**

Col Pierce de Lacy 127

THE FLIGHT OF THE WILD GEESE **129**

General Pierce de Lacy (cont) 130

Count Peter de Lacy 134

Marshal Franze von Lacy 139

Marshal Lois de Lacy 142

General George de Lacy Evans 147

James Lacy 152

J Horace de Lacy 152

Capt Patrick de Lacy 154

IN CONCLUSION **156**

Introduction

Pontefract Castle had advertised a summer picnic together with historical enactments and many other featured sideshows. A grand day out for the whole family. On arrival, my excited nine-year-old Grandson ran to look at the first information board which showed a large illustration of Ilbert de Lacy the founder of the castle.
"Grandad the man who built the castle was called Lacy too. Did it used to be our castle"?
"Of course it was" teased his mother.
Louis quizzed me as only a nine-year-old can. He wanted to know, did we (he) have a claim on the castle! There were so many more questions as the day went on about the de Lacy family. My answers were limited so I had no idea what I was letting myself in for when I promised Louis that I would research a few de Lacy facts for him...
My de Lacy quest had started!
As a child growing up in Yorkshire, I learned that Ilbert de Lacy was an aide to William the Conqueror at the Battle of Hastings in 1066. For his support, I found out that Ilbert de Lacy had been charged, with the construction of Pontefract Castle. My childish dream was that as a Lacy, I was a direct descendant of Ilbert. I later found out that the de Lacy family of Pontefract Castle died out in 1310.

Again my hopes were raised, when I discovered that Ilbert had a brother called Walter, who fought alongside him at Hastings. Walter had also, been rewarded by King William with estates somewhere on the Welsh border. Walter de Lacy's descendants had later moved to Ireland.

Both sides of my Grandparents originated from Ireland. My Grandfather Edward Lacy was born in 1862 in Dublin. Edward moved to Liverpool England, in the 1880's. For years, I knew little more than that, about the de Lacy family.

Now three years later. Louis has his answers and I am ready to share these de Lacy chronicles with you.

Once started on my research. I found over the next three years, the incredible story of an extended family, at the heart of the medieval period of English and Irish History.

The de Lacy family fighting for or rebelling against, successive English Kings. Within politics, there was a de Lacy who played a key role in King John signing the Magna Carta. In a later generation, we find much of today's laws being framed by Henry de Lacy.

Again in the Chronicles, we find de Lacy's, in a more significant involvement, this time in the history of Ireland. First, as occupying English Lords. A, de Lacy was the first Viscount of

Ireland taking lands on behalf of the English throne. Later the de Lacy family members became patriotic Irish citizens, now fighting for Ireland against the English throne.

You will find in the Flight of the Wild Geese. How in the early 1800's, members of the de Lacy family made history in their military support of different European rulers. The contents page show you why so many members of the de Lacy family deserved a role in history.

Louis now has his story of the de Lacy family, we both feel we should share the story with you Being neither a historian nor an academic, my concern was not to turn my findings into an academic dissertation. My curiosity was not into doomsday book references or reporting upon ancient documents relating to past de Lacy family members.Just satisfying the curiosity of other members of the worldwide Lacy family.

With so many de Lacy stories to tell you, the history that surrounds each de Lacy is confined to only the relevant minimum. The 164 pages of this book could just as easily been 1,164 such is the history of the de Lacy family.

The book is now also the key to the supporting website and Facebook page. You will find details at the end of the book. There you can further explore and interact with the illustrated segments of the de Lacy Barons. Facebook has Illustrated stories, and news of events posted twice a week. The address is 'de Lacy

Chronicles' You will find the website at www.delacychronicles.com.

There you will find pictures and videos etc. of all the de Lacy Castles. Our most visited page 'de Lacy Family tree'. Where de Lacy family members can interact and seek family information

The Origins
of the
de Lacy family

**Southern Scandinavia,
today's Norway**

The year was 875 AD. Harald Fairhair, the first King of Norway, called upon Jarl Rolfe, better known as Rollo the Ganger, to gather together his Clan chiefs. Among whom was Lassy, Jarl of Clan Lassy. Once the Clan leaders who had answered Rollo's call assembled, Rollo, outlined to them their mission: "We grow too many, for our sparse land. The King wants my Clan Chiefs, to decide. Do you wish to stay here fighting other Danes for the limited land available? Or seek new lands, with easier pickings.

Let me tell you, I have seen these other places on my travels and know much can be gained to enrich ourselves". Rollo so-called 'the Ganger' as he was a giant of a man. Too tall to ride the small mountain horses of the region. Rollo walked or ran into battle. Lassy and the other Clan Chiefs agreed to follow Rollo wherever he led them With a mighty roar they replied:

"We follow Lord for greater riches and greener lands."

In 879 AD, with a combined fleet of 700 longboats, they embarked on their voyage of discovery. With a collective chant that echoed around the fiord, came their new battle cry.

"Glory or the feasting halls of Valhalla is our destiny."

The River Seine, France 900 AD. In time their travels led Rollo's remaining fleet, to Northern France and the mouth of the river Seine. Their longboats carried them upstream pillaging small settlements on the way.

Having later taken the town of Rouen, they moved further inland. Until they were finally repelled by the stronger French forces intent on holding on to Paris. It was not the Viking way to lay siege. So Rollo moved further back down the river Seine. On a tight bend in the river with a good landfall, they set up their camp. From this base, they amassed great booty by demanding tolls from all boats sailing in or out, of Paris

Over the next few years, King Charles II (The Fat) tried many times to remove them but to no avail. And yet Rollo knew, this was still not the 'greener lands' he had promised his fellow Norsemen. The year turned to 911 AD. To end the stalemate, King Charles III. (Charles the Simple) Made a treaty with Rollo offering an extensive area of the French coastline where the Norseman could settle. The conditions were; leave their base on the Seine. Rollo had to marry King Charles's daughter Princess Giselle and to add the status of a Dukedom, to their new lands. Rollo and his men had to convert to Christianity thus transforming them into peaceful neighbours. All agreed to by Rollo.

Normandy 912 AD

Having agreed to the French King's terms, Rollo withdraws his army to their new homelands. They renamed the lands, Normandy, the home of the Norseman. Rollo, now the first Duke of Normandy, rewarded his loyal warlords with estates of their own. Lassy and his loyal band of clansmen received a grant of extensive lands in the hills of the Calvados region of Normandy amounting to 200 square miles. Here de Lassy and the Lassy clan members set up the family town of Lassy still a thriving if small, village to this day.

Time passed, Lassy and his followers settled into their new life. Most Norse men had followed the lead set by Rollo; they too married French woman, who introduced French culture into their homes and lives. As Christians themselves, the wives helped the conversion of the Norsemen to Christianity. Their language changed into a Norse/French dialect. The title of Clan chief disappeared, and Lassy became Baron de Laci. A name which would continue to evolve. Our de Lacy chronicle starts with Lassy's descendant

Hugh de Laci, Lassy, Normandy

On January 5th, 1066. William IV. Duke of Normandy and a descendant of Rollo, called on his principal Barons including Lord Hugh de Lacy, and his two sons, Ilbert, and Walter. The Duke excused Lord Hugh as he was now in his mid 40's, but directed Walter and his eldest son Roger, to ride to all parts of Normandy, rallying all the leading noblemen to gather ready for war on England. He charged Ilbert de Lacy, to use his negotiating talents to amass supplies and support from throughout Normandy and Brittany. Ilbert accompanied by Walter's youngest son, also called Walter. The de Lacy's played a crucial role in the preparations for the coming war with England.

Hastings England 5.30am Oct 14th, 1066.

William Duke of Normandy and his Barons stepped onto the English shore. With time to spare they disembarked the whole of the Norman army. They then made ready for the forthcoming battle with King Harold's forces. Walter and his sons, Roger and Hugh all three who had their own, commands fought under the overall supervision of Duke William's close cousin William FitzOsbern, They met the English soldiers head-on fighting with great valour in the centre of the battle. Ilbert de Lacy under the command of William's half-brother Bishop Odo leads repeated cavalry attacks on King Harold's flanks. The de Lacy family played a crucial role in the days victory over Harold's tired English army. King William, having conquered the armies of King Harold and gained for himself the English throne.

William knew full well by 1067 that he was yet to conquer England. To the West and North. King Harold may have been the King of England, but continually had to put down, fellow Anglo-Saxon uprisings outside of the old Wessex and Mercia regions. Harold had never subdued the Welsh Britton's. Even less the Jutes, Franks and Angle's along the East English Coast. In the Fens, only treaty's kept the uneasy peace. England in the North was constantly under attack by Viking raiding parties, and the Anglo-Viking population of the area were just as likely to pay homage to one leader as another.

Pontefract and Politics

The de Lacy Barons
of Pontefract Castle

Ibert de Lacy
Lord of the Honour of Pontefract
1st Baron of Pontefract Castle.
Lassy Calvados Normandy 1045, to
1093, Pontefract Yorkshire England

Ilbert de Lacy, at the request of King William, stayed behind in the North to establish a strong defensive castle to contain further rebel attacks from attempting to moving South. The castle would warn and guard against Viking invasions from the East sailing up the Humber and into the River Ouse.The key to the success of Norman conquest was their strategy of quickly building Castles within one day's march of each other. Mostly built upon suitable hilltops. Often erected within two to three weeks. The Normans made use of conscripted local labour to build a simple Motte and Bailey by digging out the sides of the hill to make it steeper and using the spoil to build a moat. Further levelling at the top of the hill, would provide a foundation upon which to build the Keep surrounded by a defensive wall of the felled tree trunks making a protective fence around the Motte. A further Bailey would be built within the security of the Outer Curtain Wall to provide living quarters. Simple to make but formidable to attack. Here the Norman soldiers could shelter and regroup before venturing further the next day.

They required only a small detachment left to defend the castle. Hundreds of such castles now appeared across England. Those built at key strategic sites with earth over rock were often developed into the castles we are all more familiar with today. Ilbert de Lacy knew the castle he had been charged to construct would have to play a crucial role in controlling all North to South movement. Instead of looking for the nearest raised ground or suitable hill, considered the usual Norman practice. Ilbert used his keen analytic mind to seek the perfect site to intercept safely all major movement between York and Lincoln.

The primary defence to entering or leaving the North was the Humber. The estuary is tidal and hazardous to ferry crossings. Ilbert considered that given sufficient warning the area could defend itself from incoming Viking longboats who could not protect themselves from onshore fire arrows. The higher reaches of the Estuary where the rivers Trent and Ouse entered the Humber covered vast areas of marsh and bog.

There were smaller routes through in the drier summer months, but again vulnerable to ambush. Ilbert reasoned 'the only safe way' to march an army and their supplies, was by keeping West, and following the old Roman Ermine Street, and crossing the River Aire, further North than the Humber. The same route King William had been guided through, on his journey to York and Durham. Ilbert de Lacy considered it to be the only feasible way for an army and all its accompanying baggage carts.

Ilbert found the perfect place for this fortification. A huge rock escarpment with two sides being a sheer drop, the other two being steep climbs to the summit. From the top the countryside spread out mile upon mile, Ilbert could even make out the smoke from many cooking fires rising to the sky; he knew it must be York. Rocks piled as windbreaks showed that they would not have been the first to use this viewing point. But Ilbert de Lacy intended to be the first to build a castle on the site.

Here he would build, with his brother Walter's help, the first Pontefract Castle. The year was 1086, by Motte & Bailey standards, it was huge, yet only a dwarf to what Ilbert had in mind. From the top of the Keep, it was possible to see as far as York to the North. To the coast and the Humber estuary to the east. The forests, stretching to the Western Mountains. Nearer to the site of the castle where Ermine Street turned to ford the river Aire at Castleford.

Perfect then, to organise defence from afar: then attack, when the enemy was near. With Ilbert de Lacy perception, Pontefract castle was to become in time, one of the important castles in the North of England. Considered the 'Key to the North' The magnificent castle, the de Lacy family, where to build. Still used to this day as a place of festival and leisure. Now held within its extensive ruins.

A delighted King William bestowed upon Ilbert de Lacy the honour of Pontefract. "The honour of Pontefract" is an irregular rectangle of twenty-five by twenty-five miles from Selby to Shipley and from Shipley to Penistone an area of 625 square miles, containing 162 Manors.

Ilbert eventually married. It was to Hawise, (family name not known) They had three children Robert de Lacy, Matilda de Lacy and Hugh de Lacy.

The practice of many Norman lords granted lands within England was to dispossess the local Anglo-Saxon Lords, replacing them with fellow Normans. Often absent, their only interest was the taxes they could collect. A practice that led to much resentment and conflict.

Having witnessed the horrors of the 'Harrowing of the North'. Ilbert visited each Anglo-Saxon lord that held estates within the Honour of Pontefract. He would allow them to retain their status on the sworn oath they gave allegiance to King William and the Lordship of Pontefract.

Collect and then pay the taxes Ilbert set as the levy on their Manor and farms. The Honour of Pontefract was now passing through a more settled time for the benefit of all.

Brothers, Walter and Ilbert de Lacy, and Walters sons Roger, Hugh and young Walter had worked together as a family unit. Now with Pontefract nearing completion as the new home of Ilbert de Lacy. Walter and his sons returned to Herefordshire where there was much to do on their new border holdings. The de Lacy's now with two English strongholds together with numerous other smaller estates. We're fast becoming a powerful Norman family. The strength of the de Lacy's was that they were prepared to work as a team when necessary. A further chronicle will unfold later in this book about the de Lacy's of Weobley Castle.

DATELINE 9th September 1087.
Normandy King William, the Conqueror died.
Succeeded, in the same year by his third son known as William Rufus. (Red Rufus)
Enthroned as King William II. of England.

At the time of the Domesday survey, Baron Ilbert de Lacy possessed 175 Lordships, the greater portion of them in Yorkshire, With others in Nottinghamshire, and Lincolnshire.

Ilbert de Lacy's youngest son Hugh entered the Clergy, to assist his son in the establishment of a new Abbey, Ilbert granted the manor of Hambleton to Selby Abbey. Hugh de Lacy became the second abbot of Selby Abbey in 1097 and held the office until his death in 1123. Ilbert also granted the manor of Garforth to St Mary's Abbey at York. He granted the funds for the church to build the chapel of St Clement, set within the walls of Pontefract Castle. Finally, then set aside land at Nostell for two separate sites for Hermits to live. This area in time became the site of Nostell Priory.

Ilbert de Lacy died in 1093 at Pontefract Castle, to be succeeded by his son Robert.

Robert de Lacy:
2nd Baron of Pontefract.
Lord of the Honour of Pontefract.
Lord of the Honour of Clitheroe.
1070 to 1129

Born 1070 at his mother's family home, Halton Castle. Robert de Lacy became one of the most powerful Barons in the North of England having remained loyal to the throne. He had twice refused to join with his cousin the Marcher Lord, Roger de Lacy in the rebellions against King Rufus. Robert de Lacy was the first Yorkshire de Lacy to found a monastery. He founded the Cluniac priory of St John the Evangelist at

Pontefract in 1090, during the reign of William Rufus. Robert dedicated it to his parents Ilbert and Hawise together with all his ancestors and heirs.

DATELINE: 1100: The death of King William II.
Succeeded by: Henry I
The youngest son of William the Conqueror.
1100 -1135

King Henry granted the Honour of Clitheroe and Blackburnshire to Robert de Lacy then added The Lordship of Bowland all of which can be found, in today's Northern Lancashire. King Henry was impressed with Robert's loyalty and wanted to improve his rather weak hold on the North West.

Within only two years Robert de Lacy had almost doubled the landholdings of the Yorkshire de Lacy family. Pontefract Castle would remain the principal seat of power and home to Robert de Lacy and his family. Robert had no intention to become an absentee Lord, leaving everything in the hands of a Chief Steward. The journey from Pontefract Castle to his Lancashire estates took many days. As Lord of Clitheroe, Robert de Lacy required an administrative centre within the Honour of

Clitheroe where he could be in residence for several months at a time.

Plans were drawn up for the second principle de Lacy Castle. It would have to be built within the new Lordship. An obvious choice was Clitheroe, in early Anglo-Saxon times, Clitheroe had been the site of a fortification or castle. The natural carboniferous limestone outcrop overlooking Clitheroe was the ideal place to build a Norman motte and bailey castle. Some material was already there from previous Anglo-Saxon forts. The wood defence walls were trees felled from the surrounding forests. For now, this would suffice till Roberts later namesake, turned Clitheroe Castle into the magnificent ruin we can still see today.

Robert de Lacy had an illegitimate son named Ralph le Rous (the red). Later, in Robert's life, he made a grant of lands to Ralph. In a charter dated 23rd Nov 1102, the estates included Great Mitton (Lancashire) Ralph and his descendants took the surname, de Mitton.

Robert de Lacy had grown powerful by maintaining King Henry's royal authority throughout the North of England acting as a go-between on the Kings behalf. This position was not to last and by 1114 King Henry fearful that Robert de Lacy was conspiring with Henry's elder brother Robert the deposed Duke of

Normandy. The fickleness of absolute Kings had a habit of quickly reversing events and in 1114, Baron Robert de Lacy was dispossessed of all his estates and sent into exile in Normandy. History does not explain why? Probably connected, with the ongoing power struggle between Henry and the Norman Lords unhappy that Henry had seized power in Normandy. King Henry I, may well have thought Robert de Lacy's sympathies had changed.

Robert de Lacy's wife was Matilda (?). They had three sons and one daughter. Their eldest son was Ilbert named after Robert's father, a second son, also called Robert, he was killed, at the Battle of the Standard on 22nd August 1138. Their third son was Henry de Lacy, who would eventually inherit from his elder brother, Ilbert (II). Their daughter was called Albreda.

Within the Honour of Clitheroe, Robert had founded the church of St Bartholomew at Colne.

Baron Robert de Lacy died about 1130 still exiled, probably in Normandy leaving his son Ilbert (II) to inherit his titles but not the estates.

Ilbert (II) de Lacy
3rd Baron of Pontefract.
1106 - 1141

On the death of Robert, Ilbert de Lacy (II)

Inherited the family titles but not the estates. The estates of Pontefract had been purchased from King Henry I, by Hugh de Lavel. To be held on a lifetime family lease. Hugh de Lavel died in 1129. King Henry allowed the marriage and its holdings to be purchased again for a considerable amount by Hugh de Maltravers

1135 King Henry I, died, his title passing to his nephew, Stephen of Blois.
Crowned as King Stephen of England
1135 - 1154

Ilbert having suffered exile together with his brother Robert was pardoned by King Steven once he came to the throne. Both Ilbert (II) and his brother Robert were granted their freedom in 1135. Ilbert regained his titles of Barons of Pontefract and Bowland. The King expressed sympathy but ruled that Ilbert's lands could not be returned as William Maltravers held them on a lifetime lease. A tenancy that King Stephen said he must honour. History records that soon after, Maltravers and his guards were returning home after collecting taxes. They encountered an unknown Knight on horseback; the Knight charged and killed Maltravers before swiftly riding off. The King's coronation took place shortly after this encounter; King Stephen restored to Ilbert de Lacy, all his family estates including Pontefract and Clitheroe Castles.

King David of Scotland declared war on Stephen

and Invaded Northumbria. Stephen marshalled a large English army and on the 22 August 1138. Ilbert de Lacy and his knights and foot soldiers fought alongside King Stephen to repel the Scottish invasion of England at the Battle of Northallerton in North Yorkshire. Ilbert took great satisfaction from routing and then defeating the Scots. Two months earlier the Scots had attacked from the West; they had killed Ilberts younger brother, Robert while attacking and looting the de Lacy estates at Clitheroe, during the battle of

England was now gripped in civil war; Empress Matilda was contesting King Stephen's right to the English throne. The Battle of Lincoln occurred on 2 February 1141. The forces of King Stephen of England had been besieging Lincoln Castle. Only to find themselves being attacked by a larger relief force loyal to and looting the de Lacy estates at Clitheroe, during the battle of Clitheroe.

England was now gripped in civil war; Empress Matilda was contesting King Stephen's right to the English throne. The Battle of Lincoln occurred on 2 February 1141. The forces of King Stephen of England had been besieging Lincoln Castle. Only to find themselves being attacked by a larger force loyal to Empress Matilda. The situation looked hopeless, most of the leading Earls deserted their King and fled.

Ilbert de Lacy, Sir Richard FitzUrse, and other men of respected Baronial families stayed and fought on; King Stephen of England was captured during the battle and imprisoned. After fierce fighting in the city's streets, Stephen's forces were defeated. Stephen was captured, taken to Bristol, and imprisoned. Effectively he had been deposed, by Empress Matilda, the daughter of Henry I.

DATELINE: 7th April 1141: Having deposed King Stephen Empress Matilda declared herself Queen of England. Unable to persuade the Church to Crown her she returned to Normandy

Ilbert had been left mortally wounded. He died leaving no heirs. After a short dispute while Matilda ruled England. The title of Lord of Pontefract Castle passed to Ilberts younger brother, Henry.

Henry de Lacy
Lord of the Honour of Pontefract
Lord of the Honour of Clitheroe
4th Baron of Pontefract.
The Entrepreneur (?) -1177.

With King Stephen in chains a prisoner of Empress Matilda. Power passed to the new Queen. Henry de Lacy suffered for the support his elder brother Ilbert had shown for King Stephen and was denied his inheritance to the de Lacy titles and estates. Henry steadfastly continued to support King Stephen.

DATELINE 1154: With all disputes now settled. The throne of England passed to King Henry II. 1154-1189

When Henry II came to the throne, Henry de Lacy received a royal pardon for anything he had done before the reign of King Henry II. The Honour of Pontefract including Pontefract Castle, The Estates of Bowland and Clitheroe and other smaller holdings that had once belonged to his father, were now restored to Henry de Lacy. Some years later while Henry was fighting an illness, he vowed that if he recovered, he would found a religious house. Having then made a full recovery Henry gave a site to the Cistercian order at Fountains Abbey to build a daughter Abbey at Kirkstall. Much of the ruins of Kirkstall Abbey still stand today, and the site has become a leisure park for the people of Leeds. The site also contains a fine the museum, telling the story of the founding of Kirkstall Abbey.

Henry de Lacy went on a crusade to the Holy Land around 1158. Returning, after only a few months. He was home, to Pontefract Castle in time to attend the dedication of the new church at Pontefract Priory in 1159. Today we might have classed that as a 'tax dodge' as he would have been exempt from all taxes for that year.

Since the days that Henry's great Grandfather, Ilbert de Lacy had built the original Motte and

Bailey castle. Pontefract Castle had continued to grow and improve through the generations. Now built strong and high with locally quarried stone Pontefract castle was a magnificent building. Like his great-grandfather, Ilbert de Lacy before him, Henry was as good at negotiating, as he was with a sword in his hand. He believed there had to be a better way to grow wealth than just take it from someone else. Until that time, it was considered that the only way to become more prosperous was by Plunder from battle or Taxation. Both of which destroyed the common man.

a license to hold a six-day fair starting on the feast day of St Giles. To be held at Pontefract Yorkshire. Having listened to Henry's ideas, the King agreed and the license, which only the King could sanction, was granted. Holding a fair or market was not new even in 1171. Most were held for one day or in major towns such as York up to two days. They were relatively local events. Henry de Lacy was thinking much bigger. The 1st Pontefract Fair was to take place over six days. It would be held in September starting on the feast day of St Giles. He realised that properly planned, the fair would bring him, as lord of the town, a great deal of money from granting licenses and concessions.

Henry sent invitations to take part or visit, to all parts of Yorkshire, Nottinghamshire,

Lincolnshire, Derbyshire and Cheshire. He promised fun, & revelry. Sporting contests for the men. Best Archer, Champion Wrestler, etc. Cookery and winemaking competitions for the Woman. For those who had reading and writing ability, there would be the opportunity to be shown how they could better themselves in trade and income. The Baron would present prizes to all the winners. Livestock sales would also take place. There would be the opportunity to trade and barter.

Henry himself would offer licenses within the honour for the purchase of mining rights in named plots. The honour of Pontefract lay within a mineral-rich area. From far and wide, the response was enormous. Ironmongers, Blacksmiths, Basketmakers, Harness makers and other tradesmen came to sell their services or wares.

Entertainers who normally went from castle to castle now demanded a license to entertain in the marketplace. Many others also requested an opportunity to trade at the fair. All could see rich pickings from a large crowd each day. The response far exceeded Henry's wildest expectations. People came from all the invited county's and even beyond. Pontefract and the surrounding villages were all packed. Every available bed space had all been booked for a good high price of course. The Inns were also fully engaged in serving food and drink. Henry realised the Inn's would not cope, sold further licences for others to set up stalls, roast meats, Ale, bread and cheese.

Many lovely young maidens were serving much more than food and ale. The street entertainers, having paid Henry for their licences made rich pickings from street collections. Some traders had done so well that they had to hire guards to escort their carts back home.

With the fair well under way, Henry was busy at the Castle with other Lords and wealthy merchants carrying out an auction for selected licences for mining rights. Henry was later fined nine pounds eleven shillings, by the King for selling these permits without permission from the King. As the sales of these alone, had mounted to hundreds of pounds, Henry was happy to pay.

Every activity of the fair had first required a paid license or royalty payment. There is no record of the actual income that went to the coffers of Henry de Lacy, but it was a considerable amount. King Henry II was delighted when he learned of the success. He understood that all the wars and battles of the last hundred years had created a dispirited nation much in need of some levity and merriment to raise the country's spirits. He urged other Barons and Earls in England to hold similar fairs. Of course, the King would also receive a percentage of their profits.

Had Henry de Lacy and his Pontefract Fair, held the forerunner, of all the County Shows, that are still held till this day?

At Easter 1177 Henry de Lacy again joined the Crusade to free Jerusalem. This time in the company of the Earl of Essex and the Count of Flanders. Henry de Lacy died while on the crusade on 25th September 1177, but how, and where is not known. Nor, whether it was by injury, or more probably ill health as he was a great age. We do not know if his burial was where he died or whether his remains were eventually brought back for burial at Kirkstall Abbey. Henry had one known son named Robert de Lacy (II) who inherited the de Lacy Lordships of Pontefract and Bowland

Robert de Lacy
5th Baron of Pontefract
5th Lord of Bowland
(?)-1193

Unfortunately little is now recorded, about Robert's life. Why did he not have to pay scutage for the 1186-87 tax year? (Tax paid by Knights and Lords for the years when not fighting for the King or the Church) There are no listed Wars or Crusades for that year.

Where necessary, I have made educated assumptions. One of the first tasks, undertaken by Robert de Lacy (II) was the extensive renovating and rebuilding of Clitheroe Castle. The Castle: was built for a purpose. An administrative centre for the honour of Bowland. Pontefract castle would remain the principal seat of the de Lacy family. Robert would only be in residence at Clitheroe for a few months of each year. With this in mind, Clitheroe was built with one of the smallest keeps of contemporary Norman castles. For the added security of this small keep, he added a curtain wall. Clitheroe Castle still stands to this day. With its now modern-day town nestling around its foundations. It is easy to imagine Clitheroe as a medieval town. Alongside the castle is an excellent museum.

DATELINE July 1189: With the death of Henry II, The throne of England passed to, King Richard I, Richard the Lionheart

Robert de Lacy married Isabella, the second daughter of Hamelin, Earl of Warenne. They had no children, and when Robert died on 21st August 1193, the lands and titles passed to his cousin Albreda. Roberts, widow Isabella, went on to a second marriage with Gilbert de l'Aigle, Lord of Pevensey. She moved to Gilbert's home at Pevensey Castle in the English county of East Sussex. There is no record to show if she had any children by Gilbert.

Even in death, Robert left questions. There are

references, stating that he had been buried at Kirkstall Abbey. As far as I have been able to find out, there are no records of that fact. If not; he was probably buried, at Pontefract. Robert and Isabella left no heir to the de Lacy estates. So ended the pure line of descent from Hugh de Lacy that had passed through his sons, Ilbert and Walter into English history.

Albreda de Lisours
Holder by inheritance of the titles)
5th Baron of Pontefract
5th Lord of Bowland)

Robert de Lacy bequeathed all of his titles to his cousin Albreda the widow of Robert de Lisours Lord of Sprotborough. Albreda was a fierce de Lacy family member. Albreda was born and grew up at Pontefract Castle. Her father had been the first Baron Robert de Lacy her brother Baron Ilbert (II). Albreda was proud that she could trace her ancestry all the way back to Lassy and Normandy.

Her daughter (also called Albreda) had married Richard FitzEustace, 5th Baron of Halton. Richard and Albreda FitzEustace had two sons. John, who was the eldest, had died in 1190 at Tyre while on a crusade. Albreda de Lisours willed her inherited titles of the de Lacy estates, to her younger grandson Roger. On the understanding that first he changed his name to Roger de Lacy and secured the continuation of the de Lacy family name before she died. preventing the estates passing to the Crown. A condition to which Roger readily agreed

Roger de Lacy (Born Roger FitzRichard)
6th Baron of Pontefract, 7th Lord of Bowland, 7th Baron of Halton, Constable of Chester
1170 to 1211

Roger de Lacy born the son of John FitzRichard. His grandmother Albreda de Lisours (nee de Lacy) had inherited the de Lacy estates, including Pontefract and Clitheroe, from her cousin Robert de Lacy. Roger had agreed to his grandmother's wishes and changed his name to de Lacy and on her death inherited all the Titles and Estates of the de Lacy family.

Besides inheriting his grandmother's vast holdings in 1194. Roger also inherited on his father's death the hereditary title of Constable of Chester. The Barony of Halton with Halton Castle and the lordship of Donington in Leicestershire.

Roger married Maud (Matilda?) de Clere about 1188. His eldest child and heir John was born in 1191. Followed by a second son also called Roger.

1191: The Siege of Acre. The port of Acre lay on a peninsula in the Gulf of Haifa. Within the modern country of Israel. On October 4, 1189, Saladin had moved to confront the encamped

Crusader army. The Crusaders now found that their camp was under siege, rather than they, besieging the port of Acre. The Crusaders fought on and stood their ground in front of Saladin's forces.

King Richard I, arrived in 1191 with an English fleet of 100 ships (which carried 8,000 men) and now with stronger leadership from Europe, it was the city and not the Christian camp that soon became besieged. While still Roger de FitzRichard he was with Richard the Lionheart on the Third Crusade he had held a command where he earned the favour and the trust of King Richard as a soldier worthy of more important commands. Roger de Lacy now considered part of King Richard's retinue. and was with King Richard when England in 1198 reconquered Normandy from the French.

Having regained Normandy, King Richard set about improving the defences. The key task was at Chateau Gaillard. Built as a massive fortification. The castle situated high on a hill overlooking the river Seine just twenty miles from Rouen. Constructed at the best strategic position to defend against an attack on Normandy. Built within two years and completed by 1198. It was one of the finest medieval castles ever built. King Richard boasted that it was impenetrable.

Dateline: May 1199, Following the death of Richard I The title of King of England passed to his younger brother. King John I (John Lackland)

Normandy in 1202; Roger based at Chateau Gaillard was in command of a hundred knights defending and controlling shipping along the Seine in defence of the French Normandy border.

Roger de Lacy stood where he regarded the best vantage point to be, taking in the whole panorama of the bend in the river Seine. Did he have a feeling of Déjà vu? Probably his Viking ancestor Lassey had stood on the same rock, taking in the same scene some 330 years in the past.

By 1203, King John was failing in his attempts to hold on to the French provinces that his elder brother King Richard had regained. Holding Normandy was now the key to also holding onto Breton and Anjou.

King John called upon Roger de Lacy, now considered his best front line military leader to take command of Chateau Gaillard and defend it at all cost against the advances being made by King Philip of France. Roger quickly asserted his authority and put in place his defensive options.

King Philip's much larger army, swooped on Chateau Gaillard. Having spent five weeks repeatedly tried to storm the defences and failing. King Philip ordered his military leaders to lay siege on the Chateau.

King Philip called for a meeting under a flag of truce with Roger. He offered Roger High Office within his Kingdom rather than remaining loyal to the weak and cruel kingship of John. Roger de Lacy rejected the terms, returning to the Chateau.

Roger was still hoping the army of King John and Earl Marshal would return to relieve them from the siege. He fought on for a further three weeks before deciding that under a flag of truce all the non-combatants, the sick the old and all the woman be allowed to leave.

Some 400 left under that flag of truce but once clear of the Chateau; they came under a hail of arrows from the French lines. They rushed to find cover in the rocks surrounding the castle. Still waiting for the return of King John and the English army. Roger knew the number of days they could hold out; he refused to reopen the gates to let them return. Both Roger's and King Philip's soldiers were forbidden under pain of death to offer any aid to them.

Roger de Lacy continued to defend the Château until every scrap of food had gone. In the end, all who remained alive, were so weakened, that the fortress was easy to overrun. Roger de Lacy had delayed the advance, of a large part of King

Philip's army. By holding Chateau Gaillard from September 1203 to March 1204.

King John never returned with his army and with the fall of Chateau Gaillard, Normandy, Brittany, Maine, Anjou, Touraine and Aquitaine were all lost within the next few months. Within only one year all the French territories that each of King since William the Conqueror through to John's brother King Richard the Lionheart had gained over two centuries were lost by King John.

Roger de Lacy was imprisoned by King Philip but treated well as he was admired, by the King, who soon released him when a ransom was paid by King John. who confirmed to him, that the honour of Pontefract was still Roger's and bestowed upon him the further offices of both Sheriffs of York and Chester. He held both until his death in 1210.

The loss of all the Plantagenets French holdings in 1204 was highly significant in French and English history. Many of the noble families including the de Lacy's had family estates in both France and England.

With no love for King John, the family members domiciled in Normandy and beyond gave their allegiance to King Philip and became French rather than Norman. The same families including the de Lacy family, having considered that their primary home was now in England decided that the only course of action was to follow suit, now declaring themselves to be English.

Again a de Lacy was at the forefront of a significant turning point in history.

Having recuperated his health, Roger de Lacy returned home to Pontefract Castle. Delighted to find the estates and castle had been well maintained, in his absence, Roger congratulated his steward on his excellent work.

Never settled and in need of a new challenge in 1205 Roger with his Knights and entourage moved on to Halton Castle from where he assured himself that his responsibilities as Constable and Sheriff of Chester were also in good order. The City and surrounds gave him no reason for concern. As Sheriff of Chester, Roger de Lacy was kept well informed about the continued skirmishes along the nearby Welsh border.

Looking for another challenge in 1205 he turned his efforts to the nearby de Lacy family's honour in Herefordshire. Much of the honour lay in disputed Welsh/English areas. The estates now administered from Longtown Castle had deteriorated as Walter de Lacy had left the running of the Hertfordshire estates to his son Gilbert. The descendants of Hugh de Lacy were now more involved in growing their massive Irish interests than being active Marcher Lords.

As Constable of Chester, Roger de Lacy could push his younger Cousin Gilbert a descendant of Walter de Lacy to better husbandry and to repel rival claims which were being pressed not only by dispossessed Welsh Chiefs but other Norman Marcher Lords, who thought the de Lacy neglected estates were now easy pickings.

While still in residence in Chester and during the Christmas of 1208, Roger earned for himself the title of Roger 'Helle' de Lacy. On hearing that the Earl of Chester was under siege by a local Welsh Army in the still being built Rhuddlan Castle, He pondered on how best to help. Most of his garrison of Knights had been given leave to return to their families for Christmas.

With the few Knights, he had at his disposal he went round all the local Chester fairs, taverns, brothels and jails. His promise of support was free ale for the whole of the Christmas festivities. The Welsh army on hearing in the night sky, the sounds of an oncoming crazy charge, by a drunken screaming force, fled in terror, their superstitious minds thinking that they were under attack by an army from hell!

Furious at the neglected English defences.Roger spent the next six months becoming the terror and scourge of the Welsh. Feared for his cruelty, during his role in their subjugation. To explain his ferocious temper and the brutal way he executed his prisoners he proclaimed he intended to live up to the name of Helle. Let his enemy beware!

Roger de Lacy died at 41 years old. November 1211 at Pontefract Castle. His remains buried at Stanlow Abbey, founded in 1178 by his father, John FitzRichard. Roger "Helle" de Lacy was one of the few Barons who had remained on good terms with King John. Roger de Lacy, was succeeded by his eldest son John.

John de Lacy
2nd Earl of Lincoln (from 1232)
7th Baron of Pontefract, 8th Lord of Bowland,
8th Baron of Halton, Constable of Chester
1192–22 July 1240

John de Lacy born 1192 at Hatton, Lincolnshire. He was still a minor when his father Roger de Lacy died in 1211. John de Lacy was a member of one of the oldest, wealthiest and most powerful Baronial families in the twelfth and thirteenth century England. The de Lacy territorial interests now distributed across all the counties of the North and the Midlands of England.

At the young age of 19, John was soon embroiled in the troubles of King John's reign. In September 1213, the King ordered him to pay a huge tax amounting to 7,000 marks (inheritance tax?) to be paid over the following three years. Payment enabled John de Lacy to retain possession of his father's estates. These comprised of over 100 knights fees, together with the Baronies of Pontefract, Clitheroe, Penwortham, Widnes and Halton. The king had pardoned John, the final 1,000 marks of his fine, for the faithful service he had received from John's father, Roger de Lacy, which he now hoped to receive from John de Lacy.

John de Lacy gave the impression of being loyal to King John. He agreed to go on the campaign to Poitou in 1214 with King John, John was one of the few Barons, to see action during the French-English war of 1212-14. At the Battle of Bouvines.

On his return later in 1214, he married Alice de l'Aigle. Their daughter Joan being their only child as Alice de Lacy had died soon after in 1216. Alice was interned, at Norton Priory in Cheshire built by Johns ancestral family the Barons of Halton.

John de Lacy like his father, Roger before him, was considered being a Baron loyal to King John. So it was with some trepidation an approach was made to him, by a small group of fellow Barons. They were seeking his support in attempting to curtail the excess of King John's tax demands on the Barons.

Holding the Baronies of Pontefract in Yorkshire, Bowland in Lancashire and Halton in Cheshire.

John de Lacy's inheritance was one of the most powerful in the North of England. What the deputation did not know, was that John nurtured a sense of grievance against the king, owing to the terms that were levied on him before King John granted him possession of his father's estates. John de Lacy agreed to join with the other Barons.

On the 25th of June 1215, King John approached Runnymede the selected meeting point, on the banks of the River Thames, near Windsor. He had a smaller than usual retinue of noblemen accompanying him, for many had made their excuses. On rounding, a bend in the track, King John's heart sank when he saw the display of power before him. Far more brightly coloured Barons tents were represented than he had expected.

King John put his seal on the charter, overseen by the twenty-five Barons including John de Lacy.

Magna Carta (the Great Charter), now agreed by King John of England at Runnymede, near Windsor, on 15 June 1215. The Charter: drafted by the Archbishop of Canterbury intended to make peace, between the unpopular King, and the rebellious Barons. The Charter promised protection of church rights, full protection from illegal imprisonment. Access to swift justice, and limitations on feudal payments to the Crown. To be implemented by the council of Barons and Bishops.

From within the twenty-five Barons, five had been chosen to oversee the observance of the charter. John de Lacy was considered the right Baron to lead this group.

Sections of the Magna Carta to this day still form parts of today's laws in many free countries.

True to his nature King John did not abide by the terms of the charter for long. Having appealed to Pope Innocent III. The Pope responded; John de Lacy learned that he had been, excommunicated along with the other Barons, who had made King John sign the Magna Carta.

King John had gathered a mercenary army and in January 1216 captured John de Lacy's reinstated Leicester castle at Donnington. He forced John de Lacy to make terms with him and to ensure John kept to the terms he had to surrender his younger brother Roger de Lacy (II) as a hostage. John de Lacy was also forced to surrender the occupancy of his castles at Pontefract and Donnington to King John, to garrison the Kings mercenary soldiers at John de Lacy's own expense.

Dateline October 1216:
Following the death of King John I, at Newark Castle. The King of England became his Nine-year-old son.
King Henry III (Henry of Winchester)

When Henry III came to the throne, John de Lacy was pardoned against all the charges made against him by King John. Pontefract and Donnington castles were now restored, to his estate. No longer a hostage, Johns brother Roger (II) returned to the family.

In 1221 John de Lacy was given by the King the role of conducting the King of the Scots, to Henry's court. For the marriage in June of his daughter Joan to King Alexander II of Scotland.

To clear himself from his excommunication, in May 1218, he accompanied Ranulph, Earl of Chester on a crusade. He was at the siege of the Egyptian port city of Damietta part of the Fifth Crusade. Later it was recorded that John de Lacy and his Knights rendered valuable service. John de Lacy having returned to England, and learned of the death of King John, offered his loyalty to the new king, Henry III, and his support to the regency of William Marshal.

While at Damietta John de Lacy made an award to establish a chapel to be built at Pontefract, in honour of the holy sepulchre and the holy cross. He returned with Ranulph Earl of Chester in 1220 and the following year he married the Earl's niece Margaret.

Baron John de Lacy married Margaret de Quincy in 1221 at Stanlaw, Chester. Margaret the only daughter and the heir of Robert de Quincy, a fellow crusader who had died in the Holy Land. Their son and heir, Edmund, was born in 1230. Daughter Maud, married Richard de Clare, heir to the earldom of Gloucester.
Margaret de Lacy's father had died on Crusade leaving Margaret heir, to her Uncle Ranulph de Blondeville estates. From this inheritance, in 1232, John became elevated to the title of the 2nd Earl of Lincoln.

John de Lacy became influential at King Henry's court and had a ceremonial role at the coronation in 1236, of Henry's bride, Eleanor of Provence.

John suffered ill health and died on 22nd July 1240. Buried next to his father, Roger de Lacy, at Stanlaw Abbey, his remains later removed to Whalley when the monks transferred there to create a new Abbey.

Although still a minor, their son Edmund de Lacy inherited the de Lacy titles. Margaret de

Lacy survived John, and married for a second time, to Walter Marshall, Earl of Pembroke.

Edmund de Lacy
8th Baron of Pontefract, 9th Baron of Halton, 9th Lord of Bowland, Constable of Chester
1230-1258

Edmund was only ten years old when his father died. He inherited all of his father's titles with the exception, of the Earl of Lincoln. For five years, his lands were administered on his behalf by the Archbishop of York. As he was a minor, his inheritance held for him in wardship by his mother. Edmund became a ward of the court and was brought up at, the royal court of King Henry III and Queen Eleanor. Edmund's education conducted by a Dominican friar named Richard Wych, who later became bishop of Chichester. Bishop Wych who later was made a Saint.

Edmund prospered well at court, and King Henry III decreed that at the early age of eighteen Edmund would succeed to all of his inheritance, without waiting to the age of twenty-one. He was now, no longer considered a ward of the court.

Arrangements for Edmund to marry Alesia, Queen Eleanor's cousin. Alesia, who was the eldest daughter of Manfred Viscount of Saluzzo (Italy), were agreed. The marriage took place in the royal palace of Woodstock. Edmund and

Alesia now retired from court life and settled at his much loved Pontefract Castle and the duties of running his vast Baronial estates.

Edmund estate duties were carried out from Pontefract Castle. For the Estates in the Northwest of England from Clitheroe Castle. A long, arduous journey over the Pennines for foot soldiers and to drive the inevitable ox carts, from Pontefract Castle. A charter granted the manor of Stanbury in 1234 together with five other manors, to Edmund de Lacy at Stanbury near Haworth. Strategically connecting the two castles with a route running from Pontefract through Bradford Dale, Haworth and over the Pennines at Colne Edge and onto Clitheroe Castle, the second Baronial seat of the de Lacy family.

An important step for Edmund. Over the following years of his life, he tended to his North West Estates as conscientiously as those in Yorkshire and the East Midlands. In 1249, on 19th December, their son, and heir, Henry was born. Later they also had a daughter, Margaret, followed by a second son John, who died in infancy.

In 1256, following the death of his mentor Richard Wych. Edmund de Lacy founded in his honour a house of Dominican Friars at Pontefract. Edmund was recorded as saying,

"I assign this place, for St. Richard, bishop and

confessor. Formerly my teacher and dearest friend, whose wish was the establishing a church on this spot, for him I lay the first stone".

Edmund made it quite clear that on his death, his body would lay at Stanlow Abbey in Cheshire The burial place of his father, John and Grandfather Roger. He had often said.

"My heart has always been in Pontefract. Bury my body at Stanlow with my kinsfolk, but leave my heart here, in the new Pontefract Dominican church".

As requested, Edmunds body went to his kinsfolk at Stanlow. Edmund having ordered, that after his death, his heart should now be buried, within St Richard's Dominican Friary, Pontefract. The six acres of land chosen by Edmund de Lacy for the Friary was named East Crofts, and in exchange, he granted 26 acres of his land to the town of Pontefract.

Edmund died the same year, on 2nd June 1258 at the age of about twenty-eight. Leaving his remaining only son, Henry de Lacy as the heir. Often given the courtesy of being addressed, as the Earl of Lincoln, Edmund never inherited the title as his mother outlived him. As the heir to his mother, Margaret de Quincy he would have only on her death inherited the Earldom of Lincoln. His father John de Lacy had only been Earl by rights of his wife's family. As Edmund had predeceased his mother, he never became the Earl of Lincoln. His burial took place at Stanlaw Abbey on the banks of the river Mersey. Edmund was at rest with his father and grandfather. Later due to flooding all of their remains were removed, to the new Whalley Abbey on the de Lacy estates at Clitheroe. Edmunds wishes were carried out, and his heart remained in Pontefract. What was important Edmund had an heir Henry, and Henry was to become the greatest of the de Lacy Lords.

Henry de Lacy
3rd Earl of Lincoln, From (1266)
8th Baron of Pontefract, 9th Baron of Halton,
9th Lord of Bowland,
1st Lord of Denbigh (from 1282)
1249 to 1311

Henry was the grandson of John de Lacy. His parents Edmund & Alesia de Lacy had both died while Henry was in his early teens. Henry was the third de Lacy heir in a row who was still a minor on inheriting the de Lacy titles. As ward to vast and significant estates, from both his father and his grandmother, he was educated at court. Both his Grandfather and Father as minors had been wards of the court. Principally for protecting their rank, titles and estates. These, however, were held at the gift of the King, who had the power to restore all or only part of the de Lacy entitlement.

Thankfully, Henry was blessed, with a strong-minded Mother and an influential Grandmother. Margaret de Quincy following the death of her husband John de Lacy 2nd Earl of Lincoln had after a period of mourning married again to Walter Marshal 5th Earl of Pembroke. On the death of Walter Marshal in 1245, Margaret (nee) de Quincy, still held the title of Countess of Lincoln and her dower de Lacy estates from John de Lacy. From her second marriage, she was also Dowager Duchess of Pembroke and had inherited a third of the Marshall fortune. Margaret was probably the wealthiest woman in England and one of the most potent.

Court wardships of leading young lords reaped rich rewards for the throne and allowed the court to dictate marital directions to other favoured titled families etc. Henry's mother had to make substantial payments to the Exchequer to keep control of the de Lacy lands and retain the guardianship of her son. To enable her to do so, she received additional financial help from Henry's Grandmother. Also, the terms agreed, still allowed. Henry's education to be at court. An unusual court arrangement for the times.

DATELINE 6th November 1272:
King Henry III died at Westminster
Edward (Longshanks) retuned from Crusade
Arriving in England in August 1274, for his
Coronation as. King Edward I.

Henry de Lacy appears to have taken over, the control of his de Lacy estates around 1271 he also inherited the title of Earl of Lincoln from his grandmother at the same time. In April 1272, Henry became the keeper of Knaresborough Castle.

Henry de Lacy was only ten years younger than King Edward, and parts of their education had been, taken together. Henry and Edward became good friends. During a private dinner together, the conversation turned to the plans that King Edward saw as his duty to accomplish during his reign. Edward put his three political goals to Henry de Lacy.

1. Bring Wales & Scotland within his reign.
2. Regain control of Gascony seized recently by King Louis of France.
3. Organise the English Justice system into a Common law that would be fair for all.

Henry considered the three points and agreed it would be a just plan, for the King. He vowed to do all that he could, to help King Edward achieve them.

By 1275, the Welsh Princes were becoming more aggressive making frequent raids on the English border. King Edward raised an Army to both repel and then conquer the kingdom of Wales. King Edward asked Henry.

"Are you happy to fight these Welsh lords some are possibly your cousins, by marriage to the old Prince Llewellyn. Do you have any kinfolk you wish me to spare"? Henry replied

"I have never met, nor know, my Welsh kin. Let us to war".

The English army curtailed and subdue the Welsh but could not conquer them. On the battlefield, the English had been held back, time and time again by the Welsh archers. Edward impressed by the Welsh use of the longbow and gave orders that they become a part, of any future English army.

In January 1278, King Edward entrusted Henry de Lacy to arrange the marriage of his daughter Princess Margaret, to the son and heir, of the Duke of Brabant. Brabant (part of modern-day Belgium) was a powerful, Low Countries province.

On Henry's return to court, the King dispatched him straight away to Scotland. King Edward I, wanted Henry de Lacy to lead the Royal party escorting Alexandra III, King of Scotland on his visit to England.

Before 1280, Henry had married his first wife Margaret Longespee, the daughter of William (III) Longespee. History is vague regarding the

Longespee family as there are three generations all called William. William (I) Longespee was an illegitimate son of King Henry II, and at one time had been designated the heir to the title of Earl of Salisbury. Following the death of her mother, the family title eventually came to Margaret making her the 4th Countess Salisbury. Henry & Margaret had one daughter Alice.

King Edward returned to Wales in 1282. This time to complete the English Conquest of Wales. Henry de Lacy again took an active role in organising the forces. For his support, King Edward granted Henry the Lordship of Denbigh. Henry immediately ordered the major reconstruction and extending of Denbigh Castle to safeguard his new estates. The old castle had been the residence of the Welsh prince Dafydd ap Gruffudd. Henry was however made himself responsible for the fortification of the town. Then at a later date the rebuilding and extension of parts of the castle. The following year, King Edward I celebrated his victory over the Welsh with a Round Table tournament at Denbigh Castle. Henry de Lacy captained the victorious team.

In 1284, Henry de Lacy became King Edward's legislative ramrod (Prime Minister?). As the King's closest counsellor, he handled the setting up, and then the steering through parliament,

much of King Edward's legal reforms. Framing regulations for the whole country, thus setting up the framework to organise a reformed national life. Much of this legislation is recognised, to this day.
Together with his chief administrator, Chancellor Robert Burnell, Bishop of Bath. Henry de Lacy spent the next five years creating new statutes and reforming others. They both oversaw these statutes passed into English law. Many of these are still in force to this day.

They included: Complete reorganisation of the fiscal system of the realm. Representation of the people: The creation of a framework to allow for the betterment and growth of Guilds, these alone, enabling the elimination of thousands of petty regulations. Henry de Lacy and Bishop Robert were also the architects of a system of courts which would be run by the people for the King, not by the King.

It was these reforms in 1290 that created the three divisions within the new legal system. They were The King's Bench, the Court of Common Pleas and the Court of the Exchequer. The framework of English law today contains elements from all three divisions. The Crown Court, The County Court and the Magistrates Court

Edward and Henry over a glass of wine one night recalled how Henry's father, Edmund had counselled both of them, saying;

"Regulation itself is not evil; only bad regulation was that".

King Edward to uphold his rights to Gascony had taken up a three-year residency there. During this time, Henry de Lacy became Chief Councilor to Edward I. He had been, appointed as the Protector of the Realm. In fact ruling England on King Edward's behalf. During the time the King was in Gascony. 1286 to 1289 Henry de Lacy repeatedly travelled backwards and forwards to Gascony.
1290 saw Henry de Lacy in Scotland as one of the commissioners appointed by King Edward to discuss with the Guardians of Scotland who would inherit the Scottish crown? Henry was present at Norham in 1291 and, at Berwick in 1292 when John Balliol was chosen to be the Scottish king.

Despite King Edward having spent three years in Gascony, no decision had been reached, as to the absolute rule of the province. During May 1293, King Edward sent Henry, together with Edmund, Earl of Lancaster, to discuss a truce with the French over the disputed lands of Gascony.

One year later, on preparing to set out on a further visit to Gascony. Henry received news that war had again broken out in Wales. Henry de Lacy rushed to relieve his castle at Denbigh. But in 1294, the castle which was still unfinished was attacked and taken by Welsh forces loyal to Madog ap Llywelyn. An English force of de Lacy Knights were defeated trying to retake the castle. However, the rebellion collapsed, and Henry escaped. Henry de Lacy within the year had retaken Denbigh. Henry stayed on in residence to ensure holding the castle and town and to oversee the continued strengthening of defences.

At this time; tragedy came into Henry's and his wife Margaret's personal life. Edmund their son and heir died. Possibly he drowned in the well at Denbigh Castle; others speculated that he fell from a turret at Pontefract Castle, No one now knows for sure but at Denbigh seems the most likely.

With the loss of his son and heir, Henry agreed to a settlement, of all his estates on the King. In return, he requested the marriage of his daughter, Alice de Lacy, to Thomas, the king's nephew. Son of the Earl of Lancaster, Henry de Lacy, reserving only a lifetime interest for himself and his wife. Henry considered this to be the most suitable way to sustain the de Lacy estates. How wrong he was!

From 1295, Henry de Lacy and Margaret spent a period as the King's representative of Aquitaine, governing this peaceful province. Henry was probably sent there by King Edward for a well-earned rest from the affairs of state and to recuperate from the loss of his son. But Henry was not a man to rest for long. During his year there, he overhauled and improved the production and distribution of the wines of Bordeaux back to London.

On his return from Aquitaine. Henry was appointed the ambassador to the French Court with the arduous task of demanding restitution for French attacks on English merchants. Later that year, Edmund Crouchback, the younger brother of the King, died. Henry de Lacy was instructed to take over Edmunds role and in 1296 appointed as the Commander-in-Chief of the English army in Gascony and Viceroy of Aquitaine.

Among his talents, Henry was an astute military leader, beating the French in 1297 when he lifted the siege on St Catherine at Toulouse, a significant military victory against the French. Again in 1297 when he then expelled the French forces from the area. Their engagement with the French army at Bourg-Sur-Mer was also successful. Moving north along the coast, they then laid siege to the town of Aux. Seven weeks later they marched South to Gascony where they laid siege to the city. Only to be recalled home by King Edward I. Lack of funds and support from many English Barons made the mission unsustainable.

By Easter 1298 Henry had returned to England. King Edward was waiting with a delicate act of diplomacy. A task, he considered would best be conducted by Henry. An arrangement was agreed between England and France to trying to end the constant, on-off conflict between England and France. Henry de Lacy had the challenge of heading the arrangements for the marriage of Edward, Prince of Wales, to Princess Isabella of France.

On Henry's return from France in May 1298. King Edward and the English army had marched North to quell an uprising in Scotland led by the legendarily William Wallace (immortalised in the 20th-century film "Braveheart"). King Edward was the overall commander, and once Henry de Lacy had arrived at King Edward's side and straight away appointed as the field commander. They engaged William Wallace at Falkirk in 1298. Edward used his longbow archers to break up the massed Scots, enabling Henry de Lacy and his cavalry to charge and defeat the Scots forcing William Wallace to flee into exile.

About this time, King Edward was making

constant demands on the English Barons for more support and increased taxes. Funds urgently needed to sustain the continuous wars waged by King Edward. This lead to, rebellious grumbling from the English Barons.

Edward knew the highest drain on resources was fighting the French. To create an alliance with the French Royal family. King Edward I, married Margaret, daughter of Philip III of France. The wedding held in September 1299 at Canterbury. Henry de Lacy 3rd Earl of Lincoln as the boyhood friend of King Edward was in attendance.

Henry de Lacy accompanied King Edward in May 1301, on a new campaign against the Scotch. Commanded once again by William Wallis, who had returned from exile. Henry de Lacy commanded the first division at the siege of Caerlaverock Castle. On the Scottish Border, eleven kilometres south of Dumfries.

King Edward instructed his Son Prince Edward, the young Prince of Wales,

"You are in overall command as suits your Royal rank. You must, however, follow without question your Field Commander, Henry de Lacy's military directions when engaging the Scotch".

The king further issued an edict. That in the event of his death. Henry de Lacy, together with the Earl of Warwick, had been appointed in advance, to hold the shared position, of Lord Protector of the realm, Regents to the Prince of Wales.

Henry's skills as an advocate and diplomat were tested in 1304. King Edward still trying to ease the tax burden imposed throughout his reign, dispatched Henry to Rome and the Vatican. Besides state taxes, all the population, were expected to pay Papal taxes to the church and Rome. Henry de Lacy negotiated with Pope Clement, a considerable reduction. Henry de Lacy received tremendous public acclaim on his return to London, Cheering crowds greeted his coach as he progressed through London.

Scottish revolt re-emerged in 1307. Robert the Bruce led an army to Ayrshire where he defeated the English forces led by Aymer de Valence the Earl of Pembroke, at the Battle of Loudoun Hill. Despite still recovering from an illness, King Edward moved the rest of his army including Henry de Lacy, North to Scotland. Several miles from the border, the King called a halt at Burgh by Sands, on July the 6th, his illness was worsening. He had developed dysentery, his condition rapidly deteriorated. King Edward died the next day, July 7th, 1307. Henry de Lacy was at the Kings bedside,

However. Henry could not prevail on the new King, to follow his father's wish regarding Piers Gaveston.

Within three months of Edward's Coronation, Piers Gaveston became reinstated at court and granted the title of Earl of Cornwall.

Gaveston's influence over the king was growing and becoming more insidious, Henry's fears over the constitutional threats to the throne also increased. During the Autumn of 1308, Henry de Lacy first drafted and then sought support from other leading Earls and Barons for the 'Boulogne declaration'. Creating a distinction between, commitment to the crown, and personal loyalty, to the person of the king. This lead to the creation of The Lords Ordainers.

The Ordainers: elected from an assembly of Lords of the Realm. Would seek to guide King Edward against his wilder decisions. They were a diverse group, comprising eight Earls, seven Bishops and six Barons, twenty-one in all. comprising both faithful Royalists and fierce opponents of the King. The clear leader of the group loyal to Edward II, was Henry de Lacy Earl of Lincoln. Henry was now one of the wealthiest men in the country. Oldest of the Earls, Henry had proved his loyalty and ability, through his long service to the King's father, Edward I. He had a moderating influence on the most extreme members of the group.

Later in 1308, Henry received a disturbing report that the grounds of Stanlaw Abbey, founded in 1178 by John FitzRichard the sixth Baron of Halton. We're suffering frequent flooding caused by Abbey's proximity to the River Mersey. The family tomb was in danger of being washed out. Henry de Lacy gave immediate instructions to build a new abbey at Whalley, North Lancashire. The new Abbey would be within the de Lacy families, Bowland estates. Henry then travelled North, to lay the foundation stone for the new Abbey church. Orders were given to transfer the coffins to the new Abbey. The coffins of Roger de Lacy, John de Lacy and Edmund de Lacy, once more came to rest, this time at Whalley.

Margeret de Lacy, Henry's wife of over 30 years, died in 1309. In a vain attempt to have an heir, Henry soon after re-married. His second wife Joan FitzMartin, sister of William FitzMartin, of the feudal Barony of Barnstaple, Devon. For Joan, this was also her second marriage. No progeny resulted from the union of Henry and Joan de Lacy. Henry's only daughter and heiress remained Alice de Lacy, who by now had married Thomas Plantagenet, Earl of Lancaster as planned.

Henry de Lacy died in February 1311 (aged around 60) at his London mansion. The growing number of Court Judges and lawyers who were establishing new legal premises in the heart of

London. Hearing of Henry's death, they named the premises Lincoln's Court in honour of Henry de Lacy. The building is still in daily use today and stands in memory of Henry's skill as an advocate. Now better known as Lincoln's Inn, one of the four Inns of Court supporting London's Law Courts.

Henry's tomb containing his remains had been in St Dunstan's chapel, within the old St Paul's Cathedral. Together his tomb and the monument celebrating his life both were destroyed together with St Paul's Cathedral, in the Great Fire of London in 1666. A new memorial erected commemorating Henry De Lacy as among the important graves lost in the crypt, stands within today's St Paul's Cathedral.
The titles of Lord of Halton, Barons of Bowland and Pontefract, Earl of Lincoln all passed in 1310 as agreed, through his daughter Alice de Lacy to Henry's Son-in-Law. Thomas, Earl of Lancaster.

The marriage of Thomas and Alice was dramatic and not a happy one. That, is, however, a story for another to tell. The de Lacy line that had begun with Ilbert de Lacy in 1066 passed to the second line with Roger de Lacy had now ended after 250 turbulent years.

Having opposed King Edward II, Thomas, Earl of Lancaster was beheaded, for treason in 1322, and his estates seized including those inherited from the de Lacy's all became Crown property.

Before leaving the Henry de Lacy Chronicle, there is one outstanding mystery to account. Many records show Henry having two sons Edmund and John. Both of whom history shows as dying while still young. What is less recorded is that Henry had another son called John de Lacy who outlived him, but he was illegitimate and ineligible to retain his father's estates.

Henry had lost a legitimate son called John. Would it have pleased him to give the same name, to a later illegitimate son? Records show that a John de Lacy inherited at that time, substantial properties in or around Grantchester in Cambridgeshire. No doubt many modern-day English members of the broader de Lacy family may have derived from this same John de Lacy.

This Chronicle has followed the male de Lacy line but should not end without paying tribute to all the de Lacy. Wives and Daughters who played their part in the successful de Lacy progression. In particular, three unyielding de Lacy woman should be acknowledged.

Albreda de Lisours (nee de Lacy) grandmother of Roger de Lacy. It was her fierce passion, for her de Lacy ancestry which made her insist that Roger, would only inherit the titles she held, on the condition, that he changed his surname, to her maiden name and became Roger de Lacy.

Without that passion, this de Lacy line would have ended far sooner.

Margaret de Lacy (nee de Quincy). The Wife of John de Lacy and also her daughter-in-law, Alesia de Lacy. Grandmother and Mother respectively of Henry de Lacy. It was their struggle with the male-dominated Royal Court which ensured that Henry continued to hold onto his full inheritance and then go on to be the greatest of all the de Lacy family.

We now step back in time to Ilbert de Lacy's brother. Walter de Lacy and the exploits of 'The Welsh Marcher Lord's, later to play a significant role in Norman Ireland

The Chronicles of Walter de Lacy and his descendants

The Welsh Marcher Lords

In recognition of their significant part in the conquest, King William 1st awarded Walter de Lacy, and his firstborn son Roger, estates throughout what is now, Berkshire, Gloucester. Worcester, Shropshire and Chester. Lord FitzOsbern had the overall task of defending the whole of the West of England including the far reaches known as the 'Welsh Marches'.

A Marcher Lord was an Earl or Baron appointed by the King of England to guard the volatile border between England and Wales known as the Welsh Marches. The name applies to Anglo-Norman lords based upon the Welsh and English border. They had total jurisdiction over their subjects, without referring to the king of England.

The Marches were a frontier society in every sense. The Marcher Barons combined the authority of a feudal lord while being a liegeman to the King. They had privileges denied to the usual English lordships. Royal rule was almost non-existent in the Marches: Marcher lords ruled their lands by their law.

Marcher lords could create their own laws, wage war, grant markets to towns, and maintain law courts. Marcher lords could build castles without seeking permission, a jealously guarded and often revoked Royal privilege to the other Norman Barons in the rest of England.

Lord Fitz Osbern soon realised that the King had

granted these lands to Roger de Lacy as a robust military warlord. He agreed that Roger de Lacy's role as one of the first Marcher Lords was to counter the border raids from the 'Wild Welsh' and then take their lands under Norman Rule. With Walter and his eldest son Roger taking on the role, Lord Fitz Osbern would have the time required to build his presence upon his greatest reward, the Isle of Wight.

Baron Walter de Lacy
1st Lord of Weobley c1038- 1085

Walters first task was to find a suitable site within the estates now in his possession and build a defensive castle. The chosen location was at Weobley in modern-day Hertfordshire. Walter organised labour and quickly built a Ring & Bailey castle, to be the de Lacy base for their border defences. Weobley Castle was within the then disputed, Welsh border region. The Castle had to be robust enough to offer security from Welsh attack. Near enough to send out raiding parties.

Here Walter together with his wife Ermeline made their English home. With them was their three sons, Roger, Hugh and Walter (II) and their two daughters Ermeline and Emma.

The third and youngest son was Walter's namesake Walter de Lacy. Even as a small child, young Walter had expressed a wish to join the priesthood, he entered Gloucester Abbey as a novice, leaving behind his de Lacy family home. In the later years of his life, his piety coupled with the education of a lord led to his fellow monks in 1130, electing Walter as the Abbot of Gloucester an office he held until his death in 1139.

It was not long before, Walter and Roger met in battle with Bleddyn ap Cynfyn, Chief of the Britons, and the people of Brecknock [Brycheiniog] and Gwent. On returning to Weobley, Walter declared, health and age had led him to the decision that his sons alone would fight future battles. Walter would continue with the building of defences and the managing of the large estates that he was amassing including the annexation of Welsh lands following the battle for Brecknock. An area which later became known as Ewyas Lacy. There he built Longtown Castle which became his home. Walter became a shrewd entrepreneur adding further holdings in Shropshire including Ludlow and Worcestershire. The de Lacy's now considered second only to the Earl of Hereford but not subordinate to him. When William Fitz Osbern son, Roger de Breteuil, The second Earl of Hereford, rebelled against the King, Walter refused to join with him, and the Earl was stripped of his title and sent into exile. The leading Baron in the region was recognised as Walter de Lacy.

Being a true Christian, Walter de Lacy was a

frequent benefactor to the Church. Making generous donations to Gloucester Abbey and founding among others St Peter's Church in Hereford In April 1084. Walter died on 27 March 1085, falling from the scaffolding around Saint Guthlac's Priory while he was inspecting the work in progress at the building at that monastery. Walter was laid to rest at Gloucester Abbey. Known today as Gloucester Cathedral.

At the time of Walter's death, he owned large estates in Gloucestershire, Worcestershire, Oxfordshire and Berkshire. Walter kept most of his manors in demesne, managing them himself rather than giving them as fiefs to his Knight followers. The Bishop of Hereford held part of Walter's, Hereford estates as a tenant. In total, the Domesday Book records show Walters lands as being worth £423 in income per year and comprising 163 manors spread over seven counties. That sum increased when including his estates in Normandy. Walter died as one of the four wealthiest men in England

The body of Walter de Lacy, Lord of Weobley was taken to the Chapter House of the Abbey at Gloucester and then entombed seven days later. Walter de Lacy was succeded by his eldest son Roger de Lacy in 1084.

Roger de Lacy
2nd Lord of Weobley
From 1085

Roger de Lacy kept his stronghold at Weobley, which he held directly from the King. From Walter de Lacy his father Roger had inherited Castle Frome, Almeley Castle, Eardisley Castle, Roger now commenced the substantial upgrading of Ludlow Castle and Longtown Castle. An insecure lordship within Ewyas Lacy on the modern-day Welsh border. These were his seats of power. Further properties in other English counties, including Edgeworth Manor in Gloucestershire and his share of the family estates in Normandy.

Roger de Lacy became a leading Marcher Lord a title given by King William I, describing Barons regarded as reliable and trusted nobles, appointed by the King of England to rule his borders, between England and Wales. How wrong this proved to be!

Roger had masterminded the de Lacy tactics of control, of their extended area of the Welsh border since the family had first moved to Weobley. A formidable soldier and tactician. He had led his Knights and soldiers in many skirmishes and minor battles with Welsh princes and leaders for over fifteen years. In this time, he was responsible for moving parts of the Welsh border ever westward. Roger de Lacy resisted counter attacks on the English border, by adding further Motte and Bailey castles. And strengthening others especially Ludlow Castle, now the de Lacy family home built in a strategic position for border defence.

As a true leader should, he had not always relied on the sword. He had become a skilled negotiator, convincing parts of Wales that they were safer, under his protection. He even added Welsh soldiers to his ranks. Roger achieved Norman, English and Welsh soldiers and servants all working together. Within his Knights, including de Lacy cousins, some had married into leading local Welsh families thus adding stability and territory.

Roger always had without question, given his oath and allegiance to King William Ist and while he loathed court attendance where he was often called upon to offer advice about the control of the West of England. So he was shocked to hear of the untimely death of the King.

DATELINE 9th September 1087. Normandy King William, the Conqueror died Succeeded, in the same year by his third son known as William Rufus. (Red Rufus) Enthroned as King William II. of England

King William had never been an intellectual King. More at home with a sword in his hand than a pen. He had never tried to merge all his conquests into one empire. Content that once conquered they be allowed to continue in isolation. With leadership under the control of family members who answered only to him.

On William's death, he considered he was giving the jewel in his crown to his eldest son and heir Robert, by inheriting Normandy and some parts of France. Robert became the 5th Duke of Normandy, considered the richer prize. His second son Richard had died in a hunting accident. Which left William's third son, William Rufus. To inherit the troubled country of England.

The news did not go down at all well with the Norman Barons domiciled in England. Being passed off by William I, with a third son rather than Robert. The Anglo-French Lords had always considered that the heir to all of King William's Kingdoms would have been first born Robert. Making matters worse, William Rufus continued to live in Normandy. For Barons like Roger de Lacy, who owned lands in both Normandy and England, it presented a difficult situation of loyalty. Two young princes had both succeeded and thus divided the lordship of England and Normandy. On hearing the news, Roger exclaimed,

"How can we serve two lords who are both different and distant from the other? If we serve Robert, Duke of Normandy, we will offend his brother, William, and be stripped of our revenues and large estates in England. On the other hand if we obey King William Rufus. Duke Robert will confiscate our inherited lands in Normandy".

Robert, Duke of Normandy was of the same opinion. He was the heir, and he should have inherited his father's entire possessions. In 1088 Robert raised a mercenary army from Normandy; Robert was intent on usurping his younger brother William and grasping England for himself.

A minority of Anglo-French Barons, including Roger de Lacy, agreed to rebel against King William and establish a united Normandy and England under one King, the eldest son & heir Duke Robert. However, most English Barons were not prepared to support this cause. Roger regrouped his Knights and soldiers, and with years of successful campaigns throughout the Welsh Marcher lands, he was able to include many Welsh soldiers. The rebellion collapsed through a lack of commitment from Robert to personally lead his army to England.

Following a failed attempt from King William Rufus to usurp his brother The Duke of Normandy. Roger de Lacy decided in 1095 that the time was right, to try once again to overthrow William Rufus. Rogers army first attacked and then captured the castle of Montgomery than the whole of Montgomery. Next Roger de Lacy overran the counties of Cheshire, Shropshire and the Isle of Anglesey. He sent one of his knights to Pontefract Castle carrying Rogers message attempting to persuade his second cousin Robert de Lacy to join with him. All he received a scathing rebuttal.

The Norman Earls, begged King William II, to return to England and put a stop to Rogers rebellion. William was both saddened and enraged at the attacks. He had always respected and compared Roger to his father William I; he had in fact considered Roger as a father figure.

Eventually, William Rufus returned to England, marching an army to the Welsh border. He attempted to engage Roger de Lacy in battle only to find; Rogers smaller Army used guerrilla tactics, much favoured by his Welsh forces. They could hold off the King's army. Roger de Lacy had made sure they only engaged the army of the King when they met in the valleys and hills.

The King's army consisted of a large contingent of cavalry unsuited to this terrain. Rogers forces would emerge and attack from the rear before the cavalry had turned and reformed the rebels had disappeared. Eventually, William gave up and built, even more, Motte & Bailey castles in his name, to stop the rebellion spreading further East into other English areas.

During this stalemate, Roger de Lacy also commanded an army on behalf of the Duke of Normandy while the Duke was absent on crusade. Roger de Lacy captured and held St

Michael's fortress against the might of the French King. He only yielded once the French discovered that water to St Michael's Fortress came by way of an underground stream and the French dug down and damned the flow of water to the fortress. Roger de Lacy negotiated with the French King an honourable draw and then withdrew. Only to be informed that his rebellion against King William II had collapsed. King William II, was now in control of Normandy as the penniless Duke of Normandy had sold the Regency of Normandy to his brother.

On Rogers return to England, William II, had him arrested. Still having a fondness for Roger King William spared his life. Roger de Lacy now stripped of all his English lands, and titles and then banished from England but allowed to keep his Normandy Estates. Little is recorded about his later life after banishment. Other than time spent managing his de Lacy estates in Normandy. Roger de Lacy died there in 1106.

Baron Hugh de Lacy
(Marcher Lord)
3rd Baron of Weobley
Died - 1121

Following the banishment of Roger de Lacy. King William II, granted in 1096, all the English de Lacy lands, including some 96 Lordships, to Roger's younger brother Hugh.

Hughes headquarters remained at Ludlow Castle. He continued amassing areas of land on the western edges of the Welsh Marches into the family's estate. He was reputed to have come across, a ruined chapel dedicated to St. David and felt inspired to devote himself to prayer and the study of St David. This moved Hugh in 1118, to found on the site in 1118, Llanthony Priory in Monmouthshire.

Hugh de Lacy had been married to Adeline (family name not known), but she died in 1121, without issue.

The next in line for the title of Baron of Weobley should have been, Walter (II) de Lacy. Walter was the youngest son of Walter de Lacy. Walter had entered the priesthood as a novice. Thus dismissing himself at an early age, from estate duties. He became Abbot of Gloucester Abbey in 1130 and was there until his death in 1139. Gloucester Abbey is now, Gloucester Cathedral

Baron Gilbert de Lacy
1104 to 1163

History agrees that the next heir to the Barony of Weobley was Gilbert, but history is at odds with itself as to the parentage of Gilbert. One version is: With the male line exhausted the titles and estates fell to Walter's daughters. First to Ermaline, but as she had no children next in line was, the younger daughter Sybil.

Sybil was the wife of Payn fitzJohn a nobleman who acted as an administrator to Henry I. Payn fitzJohn held the estates for a period but not the title of Baron of Weobley, which eventually passed to Gilbert de Lacy, a Grandson of the first Baron Walter de Lacy.

If the above explanation of the turns and twists within the de Lacy family which saw Gilbert succeed to the Family titles and estates were not enough, there is an alternative version.

Others believe (and in my opinion; correctly) that Gilbert was in fact born in Normandy, where he grew up on the de Lacy family estate. With his father, Roger de Lacy banished from England by King William Rufus. It was there that Gilbert de Lacy married Agnes (surname or parentage not known) during 1132. Gilbert and Agnes de Lacy had two sons Robert and Hugh. Both born by 1135.

With the death of King William II, Gilbert de Lacy had petitioned the new King, Henry Ist, for the recognition that he; not Hugh de Lacy was the rightful de Lacy to the estates and titles of the de Lacy family. The King rejected his claim and decreed it could not be considered again while Hugh de Lacy was still alive.

Roger de Lacy had died at the family home at Lassy, early in 1133. Gilbert inherited his father's Normandy Estates of Lassy and Campeaux. Gilbert returned to England. He felt this was the time to move to England and try to gain the title of Lord of Weobley and the de Lacy English estates. He believed the title was his, and not Hugh de Lacy's.

DATELINE 1135: King Henry Ist died,
the title passing to his nephew
Stephen of Blois. Crowned as
King Stephen of England
1135 - 1154

By late 1135 Gilbert was fighting to maintain King Stephen as the rightful holder of the title of King of England and not Empress Matilda. Gilbert had reclaimed some of his father's estates including Weobley Castle but still not the Barony of Lord of Weobley and Ludlow. Failing to get King Stephen to back his claim to the de Lacy titles. Gilbert changed sides and championed Empress Matilda in her attempt to take the English throng.

The history darkens again as Gilbert's life unfolded. Some historical accounts suggest he fought first on the side of Empress Matilda and that Matilda restored him, to the title of 4th Baron of Weobley. After which, Gilbert changed allegiance to King Stephen. Applying reasonable assumption, I doubt this later version.

Together with his cousin Geoffrey Talbot. Gilbert led his forces to Hereford in 1138 and there, following a short battle with the supporters of King Stephen took control of the town in the name of Empress Matilda. King Stephen retaliated and sent a superior force to take it back. Only by besieging Hereford for several months where the army of King Stephen eventually able to take Hereford Castle. Geoffrey Talbot and Gilbert de Lacy were able to escape and make their way to safety at Weobley Castle.

The forces of King Stephen were soon in hot pursuit. Gilbert de Lacy and Geoffrey Talbot found themselves once again, under siege. This time at Weobley. Once more they made good their escape and made their way to Bristol. They were now in an area that was under the control of Matilda's forces.

DATELINE: 7th April 1141:
Having deposed King Stephen
Matilda declared herself Queen of England.
Her contested reign continued only till Nov 1141.
Unable to persuade the Church to Crown her, Matilda returned to Normandy.

By the late 1140's Gilbert de Lacy had recovered most of the remaining de Lacy Estates, which had passed from his father Roger to his Uncle Hugh de Lacy. But despite carrying the title of Baron, he had not been able to regain the full title he coveted of Lord of Weobley.

DATELINE 1154: With all disputes now settled.
The throne of England passed to:
King Henry II.
1154 - 1189

In, thanks: Gilbert de Lacy gave land for the building of a Cathedral chapter for Hereford Cathedral. To the Knights Templar, he granted a Manor at Guiting in Gloucestershire. Gilbert also provided funds towards the construction of a church at Weobley.

Though having gained back his estates, Gilbert remained disillusioned that having partitioned three Kings, he could not regain the title of Lord of Weobley; the title stripped from his father. In 1158, he made a momentous decision. He surrendered all of his hard-won lands to his son Robert.

Gilbert de Lacy had decided to turn his back on England and went South becoming a member of the Knights Templar. He travelled through France on his journey to Jerusalem. Through the following five years, he was elevated to the office of Precentor of the Templars at Tripoli on the Lebanon/Syria border. A position, demanding much learning and executive ability, his standing and dignity corresponded with his duties. During 1163, he was reputed to have been among the leaders of a Crusader army resisting the Turkish Muslim leader.Nur-ad-Din. The year he died is not known.

The history of Gilbert started with the puzzle surrounding his entitlement to the title of Lord of Weobley. That he was of the de Lacy bloodline is not in doubt. Was it of the male line or the female line? We favour the male line; Gilbert, son of Roger. Records are unclear whether Gilbert ever received the full title to which he considered he was entitled.

His son Robert de Lacy had predeceased him dying without children in 1162. The de Lacy Inheritance now passed to Gilberts youngest son Hugh de Lacy
The Marcher Lords, based on England's troubled, ever-changing Welsh border, were rightly viewed as War Lords. Each paying scant compliance to English rule. Successive Kings were prepared to accept this, as it kept the Welsh at bay, with little cost to the Throne. This left the Marcher Lords record keeping, more obscure than in other areas of England.

DATELINE 1154:
The vacant throne of England was filled by:
Henry II 1154–1189

Baron Hugh de Lacy
4th Lord of Weobley. 1st Lord of Ludlow
Born at Ewyas Lacy 1135-1186

With his brother Robert, Hugh de Lacy continued building the growth and affluence of the de Lacy estates in and about Herefordshire and Shropshire. On the death of Robert in 1162. Hugh took full control of the properties without holding the title, until the death of his Crusader father, Gilbert de Lacy.

During this time, he restored land lost to local Welsh chiefs and other Marcher Lords. Including Ludlow Castle. He improved the yields and wealth of the many manors, held within the de Lacy estate. Restoring incomes to a level equal to his Great Grandfather Walter de Lacy holdings. In recognition, King Henry II returned to Hugh the long-suppressed title of Lord of Weobley. Hugh became the 4th Lord of Weobley holding the entire de Lacy estates. King Henry additionally appointed Hugh de Lacy as Lord of Ludlow.

Hugh de Lacy married Rohese of Monmouth, about 1155. (also known as Rose of Monmouth). She was the granddaughter of Gilbert Fitz Richard. Hugh now one of the most powerful Marcher War Lords. Not since the days of his Grandfather, Roger de Lacy, had the name of de Lacy held more fear or respect in the West of England from Anglo-Normans, and Welsh alike.

In 1171, Hugh travelled to Pontefract in Yorkshire at the request of his Cousin Henry de Lacy. Henry wanted to discuss what his cousin's reactions would be if Hugh was summoned by the King (Henry's friend), to accompany the King on an expedition to Ireland. On the expected success of the invasion, Hugh would take up residence as the Kings Viceroy in Ireland. Henry de Lacy knew only too well the reputation of the Marcher Lords and their independent attitude. He did not want to see King Henry being met with a rebuttal. Henry did not need to worry; Hugh always ambitious would be delighted to accept, should the offer follow from the King.

Passage to Ireland

It was inevitable that France or England would eventually attempt to expand their respective kingdoms by the occupying of Ireland.

The Ireland of the mid-12th Century was not a united country, having many smaller kingdoms loosely ruled over by a not so secure High King. Leading to constant conflicts breaking out between one Irish King at war with another.

Henry II had received in 1155 a letter and a ring as a symbol of investiture from Pope Adrian IV granting the English King the lordship of Ireland. Pope Adrian IV had authorised Henry II of England to claim Ireland as part of Henry's Kingdom to reform the Church and bring it in line with current Rome instructions. Only one year into his reign and still coming to terms with the problems he had inherited throughout his French and English territories. King Henry decided these concerns must take precedent before he further extended his rule. No! Ireland must wait.

With other events taking the precedent, it took over 20 years before Ireland became an issue for the King. For Henry, the time was still not right. His hold over England was even now not secure. The last thing Henry wanted was to start an expensive war.

Dermot MacMurragh, the ousted King of Leinster, came from Ireland seeking help from King Henry II to regain his crown. King Henry was reluctant to offer any support. As a compromise, he permitted MacMurrage to attempt at his own cost raising a mercenary army made up of such Norman lords and others he could find.

Dermot MacMurragh returned to Ireland in 1169. He had enlisted support from several Anglo-Normans Barons, the principle of these was the Marcher Lord, Richard de Clare, the Earl of Pembroke, often called "Strongbow" the rest of his army comprised Welsh mercenaries.

King Henry II had disliked the Earl of Pembroke (Strongbow) ever since he had opposed Henry in his bid for the English throne. He was not welcome at court, and King Henry had excluded him from English affairs.

Once in Ireland, the Anglo-Normans aided by the Welsh mercenaries quickly seized Leinster. Strongbow then set about launching raids into neighbouring kingdoms. By May 1171, Strongbow had assumed full control of Leinster and had conquered the territories of Dublin, Waterford, and Wexford.

Dermot MacMurrage now reinstated, had promised Strongbow, his daughter Aoife in marriage, together with the Kingdom of Leinster upon MacMurrage's death. He hoped to keep the ongoing support of Strongbow in Ireland. With little prospects in England, Strongbow was quick to accept.

The situation changed suddenly in May 1171. King Dermot died, Strongbow, as agreed, now crowned as King Richard of Leinster. When word got back to King Henry of England, he was furious. He had given permission. To help MacMurrage, not to put Strongbow in a position of power to rival his authority as King.

Early in 1171, King Henry realised he must now exercise the symbol of investiture from Pope Adrian IV, and subject Ireland to English rule. He requested his loyal friend Henry de Lacy should accompany him in the Invasion and once Ireland fell. Henry would become The Kings Viceroy. Henry de Lacy pleaded not to be given the task, due to his advancing age and the need to groom and prepare Robert de Lacy to become the Lord of Pontefract. He advised his King that a far better man for the role was his nephew, Hugh de Lacy. The King agreed. At the appropriate time, he would appoint Baron Hugh de Lacy of Weobley as his first Viceroy of Ireland.

In October 1171, King Henry accompanied by Hugh de Lacy landed a large army at Waterford in Southern Ireland to establish control over both the Mercenary-Normans and the Irish. The Norman lords handed their conquered territory to Henry. They realised that the King could, and would defeat them, Strongbow, (Richard de Clare, 2nd Earl of Pembroke) intercepted Henry at Waterford offering his apologies and begging forgiveness. Henry's anger must have subsided as he relented allowing Strongbow to remain,

Lord of Leinster as a fiefdom, providing that all the towns taken were now to be considered Crown land. Strongbow accepted and submitted to the authority to the King of England.

The less powerful Irish Kings of Munster Breifne, Airgialla and Ulaid also decided that rather than face a bloody battle, they were better off swearing tribute to King Henry enabling them to hold on to their lands.

High King, Ruaidrí Ua Conchobair (Rory O'Connor) of Connacht, and the Kings of the Northern Uí Néill refused to submit straight away to King Henry. Early in 1172, Hugh de Lacy as the King's representative started negotiations with Rory O'Connor, High King of Ireland for his submission to the Throne of England. It was not till 1175 that Hugh was to succeed in his negotiations.

However in 1172 King Henry II, had straight away granted, the unconquered kingdom of Meath and fifty of his knights, to Hugh de Lacy. On his investiture as the First Viceroy of Ireland, Hugh became the custodian of Dublin Castle now declared the official residence of the Viceroy.

The de Lacy family were in Ireland and to stay!

Baron Hugh de Lacy.
At Trim Castle Ireland,
1st Viceroy of Ireland, 4th Lord of Weobley,
1st Lord of Ludlow 1st Lord of Meath.
1135-1186.

Hugh now returned intermittently to Ludlow Castle. In 1173, he was in Normandy, fighting Louis VII of France on behalf of Henry II. On his return from France, Hugh returned to Ireland to the neglect of his Marcher estates. A pattern continued with following descendants of Hugh. There was still unfinished work that needed attention on the family border estates.

Around, 1175 Hugh de Lacy eventually gave orders for the re-building of Longtown Castle in West Herefordshire. The castle, originally built with earth and wood on the site of former Roman earthworks, was now reconstructed in stone The builders made use of the existing man-made motte, or mound, possibly Iron Age in origin. The new castle design was unusual having three baileys and two large enclosures enabling the security of the de Lacy's and the neighbouring town.

Here then, whenever in England would be the new, Herefordshire seat of the de Lacy's. Replacing the smaller Weobley Castle, which was not suitable for expanding into a more significant status site. Together with the retained Weobley and newer Ludlow Castle,

Hugh considered his Welsh-English borders would now be well protected while he was absent. In Ireland Baron Hugh de Lacy now Lord of Meth, made sure that he was the personal overseer of his more critical building project, Trim Castle.

Hugh set about building a defensive Irish castle in the best available strategic position available to him. Enabling the maximum control of his far greater new lands of Meath. Land granted to him by King Henry II. The site was on the south bank of the River Boyne at Trim, County Meath, Ireland. Trim Castle, or called by the Irish: Caisleán Bhaile Atha Troim, was built as a larger than average ringwork castle.

Defended by a substantial double palisade with an outer ditch at the top of the hill. In all a total area of 30,000 square metres, it was, and still is the largest Anglo-Norman castle in Ireland. Improvements continued without pause over the next 30 years, Hugh de Lacy, followed by his son Walter kept extending and improving the seat of the Lordship of Meath.

Hugh and the boy Walter stood one evening by the newly built ramparts of Trim Castle Hugh instructed his son:

"You were born at our family's castle at Weobley, but Walter, you have not witnessed what I have seen. I visited our Uncle Henry, at Pontefract in Yorkshire. Even after 100 years,

our cousins are still building Pontefract castle making it one of the finest castles in England. Walter, Trim Castle is now becoming the third principle home for the de Lacy family. Should anything ever happen to me, you must continue making Trim Castle the finest in Ireland".

Trim castle now became the centre of Norman administration for the Lordship of Meath. Hugh's son Walter kept his promise and continued rebuilding. The castle was finally completed c1224.

The granting of Meath to a Norman Lord was not acceptable to Tighearnán Ó Ruairc, King of Bréifne, who ruled Meath. Ó Ruairc refused to give up the land. He demanded a meeting with Hugh de Lacy at Meath. A dispute ensued in which Hughs interpreter while deflecting a blow aimed at Hugh de Lacy was himself killed; Hugh fled the scene; Ó Ruairc was killed by a spear-thrust from one of Hugh's knights. Ó Ruaircs head was taken back to Dublin and impaled over the gate of Dublin Castle.

Hugh returned to England, and on December 29th, 1172 was present at King Henry's court. Enraged at the scorn Archbishop Richard of Dover, was pouring on the Irish people. He was calling them backwards savages, not fit hold their lands. Hugh rounded on the Bishop. Who had never been to Ireland, and with a voice loud enough to alarm the whole court, shouted *"you are a fool sir and know nothing about the Irish"*.

Later that day, King Henry called Hugh and told him:

"I am about to leave for France, to engage Louis VII. He has invaded my lands yet again, and I must retaliate. Hugh, you have upset the whole court with your outburst at the Archbishop of Dover. I think it would be better if you accompany me on my expedition to France".

Hugh returned to Ireland in early 1177, having been installed by King Henry as procurator-general. The grant of Meath now confirmed, with the further addition of Offaly, Kildare, and Wicklow.

As governor of Ireland in the King's absence, Hugh now ensured the security of both Meath and Leinster, Strongbow having died the previous year. Hugh had ordered the construction of numerous castles in all troublesome areas, to control both regions. He also instigated the setting up of the feudal system, allowing the Irish to hold tenure of their lands.

King Henry II, granted Baron Hugh de Lacy 'the lands of Meath', from the Irish King Murchadh, now to be held "as high as anyone before or after him that had ever held it." This grant, known as a Liberty, gave Hugh de Lacy power equal to that of the king himself, the only reservation being that only the king could dispose of Church lands. By 1177, the Anglo-Normans were now fully instated at Leinster and Meath. The Liberty of Meath continued under the rule of Hugh de Lacy while also governing The Lordship of Leinster on behalf of the Crown.

One of the privileges of a Count Palatine was that Hugh de Lacy could now create Barons or lesser Lords. Hugh divided his lands among his newly created Barons who would rule under him. At least three de Lacy cousins became Barons. Subject only to the Lord of Meath and the King.

Later King Henry II adopted a new policy. He declared his youngest son, Prince John, to be 'Lord of Ireland' (i.e. of the whole island) allowing the Anglo-Norman lords to conquer new Irish lands. The territory they held became the Lordship of Ireland and formed part of the Plantagenet Empire.

Hughes first wife Rohese died before 1180. She had born Hugh nine children, four sons, and five daughters. They were:

Walter de Lacy (1166–1241). Hugh de Lacy, 1st Earl of Ulster (bef.1179–1242). Gilbert de Lacy (No known records found). Robert de Lacy (died young). Aegida de Lacy married Richard de Burgh. Elayne (Elena) de Lacy, married Richard de Belfour. Alice de Lacy, who married Roger

Pipard, then married Geoffrey de Marisco, Justiciar of Ireland. Daughter de Lacy, (name?) who married Sir William FitzAlan, Lord of Oswestry.

In 1181, Hugh was again in trouble with King Henry and recalled to England. Without the King's permission, he had re-married to Princess Rose Ní Conchobair, daughter of the deposed High King of Ireland, Ruaidrí Ua Conchobair. The marriage never to be recognised, by King Henry II. but the significance of the wedding caused concern. King Henry had not forgotten The marriage without his permission of Strongbow in 1171.

This second Anglo/Irish marriage further reinforced King Henry's suspicions that Hugh de Lacy may now try to establish an Anglo-Norman independent state in Ireland. Hugh and Rose had two children, a son and a daughter: William Gorm de Lacy (who was declared illegitimate by Henry II of England) and Ysota de Lacy.

By the following winter, Hugh was granted permission to return to Meath. Hugh was of more value to Henry in Ireland, then being a thorn in Henry's side at court.

Early in 1185, Prince John visited Ireland, the young prince complained to his father King Richard I, that Hugh de Lacy would not permit the Irish to pay tribute to him. Leading to further disgrace, at court. This time, Hugh stubbornly remained in Ireland. He continued to occupy himself as before, with castle-building

Coming to Ireland as an Anglo-Norman, Baron Hugh de Lacy had fallen in love with the country and yet in his unforgiving Norman style; he earned the reputation of being a harsh master. In his latter years, Hugh de Lacy became unloved in both England and Ireland. Henry nevertheless had carved out a solid foundation for the Lacy family in Ireland. Meath was now highly productive, filling many of Hugh de Lacy's cargo ships with grain to sell throughout England and Europe.

Hugh had introduced the Norman feudal manorial system into Meath. The income and it was a vast income, primarily going to Hugh's coffers. Next, to those people who now had tenancy granted to one of the Meath Manors. The Irish peasants who farmed the land saw little of it!

While overseeing the construction of a Motte & Bailey castle at Durrow, Tullamore in 1186 Hugh de Lacy was murdered by a local Irish chief, Gilla-Gan-Mathiar O'Maidhaigh, who delivered a swinging sword blow severing Hughes' head.

On hearing of his death, King Henry immediately sent his younger brother, Prince John to Ireland to take possession of all of Hugh's lands in the King's name.

DATELINE 1189: With the death of Henry II, the throne of England passed to, King Richard I, Richard the Lionheart

Hugh de Lacy was initially buried at Durrow Abbey. Only for his body to be disinterred in 1195 by the archbishops of Cashel and Dublin. They buried his body in Bective Abbey in Meath and his head in the tomb of De Lacy's first wife, Rohese at St. Thomas's Abbey, Dublin. Hugh had been a benefactor of Llanthony Abbey in England, and including many churches in England and Ireland, including Trim.

Walter de Lacy.
5th Lord of Weobley. 2nd Lord of Ludlow
2nd Lord of Meath Born 1172:
Weobley Castle Ewyas Lacy, Herefordshire.

Hugh de Lacy,
Brother to Walter
Earl of Ulster, Born 1176:
Weobley Castle, Ewyas Lacy, Hertfordshire.

William Gorm de Lacy
Half Brother to Walter & Hugh
Born 1180: Longtown Castle, Ewyas Lacy Hertfordshire

While all three sons, of Hugh de Lacy Lord of Meath, deserve their place within this Chronicle. Reading their stories together makes better sense.

In 1186 at the time of his father's death, Walter

still a minor did not succeed to his father's estates in England, Wales and Normandy. Nor become Lord of Ludlow and Weobley until the latter part of 1188. Taking possession of the Irish estates as Lord of Meath, after considerable political and personal arguments with not one, but two Kings.

Walter de Lacy had to pay (expensive) homage to King Richard; this was for the recovery of the de Lacy estates in Ireland. Walter finally received during 1194, the Lordship of Meath previously held by his father, Hugh de Lacy.

Hugh de Lacy, the younger son of Hugh de Lacy Lord of Meath, had been given the position of Coadjutor (Principal aide) by King Richard. It was to a leading Anglo-Norman Baron, John de Courcy who had estates in Leinster and Munster. The post proved to be a disaster as bitter rivalry had broken out between them. Hugh disagreed with de Courcy ambitions.

About, this time, Hugh de Lacy (II) married his first wife, Lesceline de Verdun. Unsubstantiated accounts say he abandoned her a few years after the marriage. Or possibly she died, the records are incomplete.

During the revolt of Prince John Lackland, Lord of Ireland, against his brother King Richard. Walter felt it would be wiser to give his support to King Richard I. During the 1193-94 revolt, Walter captured, a party of Knights loyal to

Prince John. They had been escorting Peter Pipard, Prince John's, Justiciar (Governor) in Ireland.

Walter, married Margaret de Braose, the daughter of William de Braose of Brecknock, the 4th Lord of Bramber in November 1195. The de Braose family seat situated in the Horsham area of West Sussex. Like the de Lacy's they had their most significant estates and most powerful influence on the Welsh-English border and in Ireland, including Limerick.

The downside of the de Lacy de Braose relationship was the King's suspicions of the powerful Marcher Lords allying with their holdings in Ireland, besides their firm grip on the Welsh England border. The King's suspicions and his fear of loss of control further reinforced by this family merging its interests.

Again in 1197, Walter had to offer further payments to King Richard. This time to try to re-recover his Norman and English lands. The King had sequestrated both, possibly for actions taken by Walter, to increase his, de Lacy holdings in Ireland. More likely because the de Lacy, de Braose connection appeared to King Richard, to be too strong. Walter possibly seen the weaker of the two lords.

DATELINE 27th May 1199: John Lackland: King John I third Plantagenet King (He reigned until 1216)

Upon taking the throne of England in 1199, King John wrote to his justiciar in Ireland. The King complained that de Courcy and Walter de Lacy had destroyed John's land of Ireland. Walter was, therefore, to be considered an enemy of King John.

John de Courcy had assembled a personal army and swept through Northern Ireland invading and taking Irish Kingdoms. All this was without seeking permission from Prince John. Although being Lord of Ireland, Prince John and had little knowledge of what was happening there. Upon being crowned; King John became enraged to discover then that John de Courcy had authorised the issuing of new coins into Ulster. One side of the coin depicted St Patrick the other, the head of de Courcy. This act was seen by King John as a clear usurpation of his rule.

In 1199, King John of England gave Hugh de Lacy the authority and resources, to raise an army and wage war on John de Courcy. In 1203, Hugh de Lacy and his brother, Walter, led a raiding force into Lecale and attacked, de Courcy in Downpatrick. By supporting his brother, Walter hoped to find King John's forgiveness.

King John in 1203, granted the custody of the city of Limerick to Walter's father-in-law, William de Braose. As de Braose was absent, tending to more pressing affairs on the

Welsh/English borders. William de Braose asked Walter to serve as his deputy and govern Ireland's second city Limerick, in his place. Hugh de Lacy had John de Courcy on the run, so Walter could leave Hugh, and to accept the offer to move to Limerick, to act as Governor.

Hugh had proved himself to be a capable leader and by 1204 had defeated John de Courcy, taking occupation of all his lands in Northern Ireland. The defeated de Courcy now transferred to the care of the King's officers, and a delighted King John had de Courcy stripped of his titles and sent into exile.

Early in the new century, Walter de Lacy finished re-building Longtown Castle in Herefordshire. Using this time, stone not wood and earth. Built with a circular keep erected on the Motte for the grand sum of £37. The local area became known as Ewyas Lacy.

At court in May 1205, King John rewarded Hugh de Lacy with a charter granting him land in both Ulster and Connaught. Together with the estates granted, Hugh was also raised to the peerage as the Earl of Ulster. On King John's return to Ireland later in 1205, he appointed Hugh de Lacy as the new Viceroy of Ireland. The Earl of Ulster had become the most powerful Lord in Ireland.

The same year 1205, Walter de Lacy's wife Margaret gave birth to their son Gilbert who became the heir to the title of The Lordship of Meath.

Nothing stays the same for long for the de Lacy's in Ireland. King John had a change of plan and removed the title of Viceroy of Ireland from Hugh de Lacy. In 1206-07, Walter became involved in a dispute with Meiler Fitzhenry, King John's new Governor of Ireland; The argument was over, Walter's refusal to collect King John's new feudal levy on his tenants land in Meath. Meiler reaction was the seizing of Limerick in the King's name. That Walter was only acting Governor on behalf of William de Braose appeared to make no difference to Meiler Fitzhenry.

Walter's younger brother Hugh de Lacy, 1st Earl of Ulster, had then taken Meiler Fitz Henry a prisoner in retaliation. King John had no desire to be in a conflict over Irish affairs, with two de Lacy's at the same time. To split the two brothers apart King John summoned Walter during April 1207, to appear before him in England. So in March 1208, he sought Walters support and in return, granting Walter de Lacy a new charter for his lands in Meath.

Returning to Ireland later in 1208, Walter (may have) acted for King John as Justiciar (Governor) of Ireland as Meiler Fitz Henry, had now been deposed.

Walter had never forgotten his pledge to his

father to build Trim Castle to rival Pontefract Castle in Yorkshire. During this time, he commissioned the quarrying of more stone, ensuring the continued growth of the fortifications at Trim Castle by rebuilding a massive Curtain wall.

In 1210, war broke out. Hugh Earl of Ulster and other leading Anglo-Norman Barons were rebelling against new laws and taxes imposed by the King's latest justiciar (King's Regent). King John was again forced to make his second journey as King to Ireland.

On the 20 June 1210. King John landed at Crook, which is now part of Co. Waterford Ireland. With him was an army of Flemish mercenaries. King John was intent on establishing his feudal levy throughout Ireland, by force if necessary. Marching north, through Leinster they reached Dublin within a week.

When William de Braose rebelled against the King and then fled across the Irish Sea, King John suspected Walter of involvement. King John attacked Walters lands in Eastern Meath. Four hundred of Walter de Lacy's fighting force deserted him to join King John's mercenary army.

King John's first act following his occupation of Dublin was to expel Walter de Lacy once again from Meath. Meanwhile, Hugh de Lacy fearing for his life fled to Scotland.

Walter threw himself on King John's mercy, sending five of his tenants to Dublin to place his lands in Meath in the King's hand. Walter tried to assure King John that he had not tried to shelter his brother Hugh from John's wrath. King John would now hold Walter's lands in Meath. King Richard had done the same in the past making this the second time that Walter de Lacy had surrendered de Lacy estates to the Throne this time for five years.

By 1215, King John was desperately seeking support from Ireland, against the growing rebellion of Barons throughout his English domains, ending with King John signing the Magna Carta. King John having first exacted a hefty financial penalty from Walter de Lacy, promised the return of all his lands for this support.

In the summer of 1215, King John had made good that promise and returned all of Walter's lands in Meath. By the autumn, Walter de Lacy now restored to favour at King John's court. King John had also issued a pardon to Hugh de Lacy, who now returned from Scotland, knowing that he still held the office of the 1st Earl of Ulster.

With Walter trying to improve the dwindling incomes from the Ewyas Lacy estates that had fallen desperately low due to his poor stewardship of politics, poor harvests and the

Kings fines had also reduced Walters overall income. Walter had become an absent landlord at Weobley and Longtown and now as he was expected to attend more frequently, King John's depleted court, Meath and Trim Castle. More powerful English Barons were staying away from the unpopular King John. The irony of this situation was that having recovered Meath, he could no longer reside there. In his absence, Walter installed in 1215 his younger half-brother William Gorm as custodian of Trim Castle and steward of all the de Lacy family's Irish estates.

*DATELINE October 1216:
With the death of King John I, at Newark Castle. Throne of England passed to his Nine-year-old son. King Henry III (Henry of Winchester)*

1216 was a time of turbulence both in England and Ireland. William Gorm de Lacy was involved fighting both Norman and Irish armies in a succession of small Irish wars that had broken out. More Norman Lords entered Ireland trying to take the land. Irish chiefs saw these troubled times as an opportunity to regain lost property, or even add more. The original Anglo-Norman families saw themselves vulnerable following the unrest created by the death of King John, and the installation of a nine-year-old boy to the English throne.

William Gorm had built a formidable army of

Meath Knights and foot soldiers feared all over Southern Ireland. William had added more land to the de Lacy estates, by taking the castles and lands of Rath and in the North Carlingford.

Walter's continued absence, trying to hold on to the de Lacy Marcher estates in England led to the dwindling of the vast income that Walter's father had created in Ireland from the large Meath Estates. William Gorm was a warrior and not an estate manager. Holding Trim and retaliating to the ravages of war continued to be his primary concern. Not, how well, the crops were faring.

Heavy continuous rainfall in The spring of 1315 led to problems for Irish farms. Seeds rotted in the ground leading to a reduced harvest. The Irish peasants reduced to grubbing for berries in the forests to bulk out their meagre harvest. There were few deaths that year but with the same weather problems in 1316 and again in 1317 leading to many people dying of starvation. By 1317, all classes of society became affected. Meath having a large well-cultivated area with many mouths relying on its produce felt the full effect of the famine more than the less cultivated regions of Ireland. Things were no better on the de Lacy English estates which also suffered themselves from 'the great famine of 1315-17.

In 1217, William was ordered to give up the

custody of Rath and Carlingford Castles, to the Justiciar Geoffrey. de Marisco who had been appointed previously by King John. William also had to make reparations to the Justiciar for the damage done to both King John and the English throne, by capturing these castles. Newly crowned King Henry III decreed that as the Lord of Meath, in July 1217, Walter de Lacy should be made to stand surety and vow that he would make amends, for William's excesses towards the King.

After his long absence, Walter de Lacy finally returned to Ireland in 1220. During the following years, he was engaged together with his brother William Gorm in a continuous series of minor wars and skirmishes both with fellow Anglo-Normans and Irish clan chiefs. Not for the first time, and not for the last, these were troubled times in Irish history.

Hugh de Lacy had returned in 1221, to Ireland having taken part in King Henry's war in France. He now allied himself with the powerful Irish O'Neill family past Kings of Northern Ireland and still antagonistic towards English rule. Half Irish, William Gorm de Lacy also had little love for any, English King was ready to assist Hugh in his Irish plans.

During 1223-1224. Dublin was rife with civil disobedience and corruption. Henry of London, the Bishop of Dublin, was the King's appointed justiciar but had remained complacent to the corruption. A representative of not only the Church and the Crown, but also a Merchant and Landowner, which led to his lax rule. Fearing the possibility of attacks on Dublin, he had been granted extra funds by the King to fortify the walls of Dublin Castle, which he had neglected to do.

Hugh de Lacy on returning to Ireland in 1221 attempted to re-establish his position in Ulster by force of arms. Walter could not restrain his half-brother William Gorm nor stop many of his Meath knights from rising to support Hugh de Lacy. Hugh had realised that he had much to gain and little to lose. With now with the backing of his Irish friends the O'Neill's and including the knights and foot soldiers who had joined him from his brothers Meath Estates. Hugh de Lacy had raised an army.

Now assembled Hugh de Lacy's army, marched in 1223 on a frail Dublin City. Henry of London, realising his Dublin defences would not hold sued for a truce till the following summer. King John unable to come to Dublin's aid. Called upon Hugh, to abandon his campaign. In return, King John restored to Hugh de Lacy the Title of Earl of Ulster and all the lands and estates that went with it.

Meanwhile, William Marshall the Earl of Pembroke, reported to Henry III King of England,

That in 1224, he had besieged Trim Castle while it was still under the command of William Gorm de Lacy. Marshall had stormed and with some difficulty, take the castle. Only to find William Gorm de Lacy had escaped.

The eldest daughter (name not recorded) of Earl Hugh and Lesceline de Lacy was given in marriage to Alan Fitz Roland Lord of Galloway in 1226. Alan was the hereditary Lord of Galloway and Constable of Scotland Thus linking two of the most powerful families in Ireland and Scotland. By this time Hugh de Lacy was no longer living with Lesceline leading the society gossip of the day to be that Hugh now lived an adulterous life

By 1227, William Gorm became reconciled with King Henry III and entered the King's service on a grant of £20 per year. His role was to lead battles in the King's name within Europe.

Hugh de Lacy as Earl of Ulster also reverted to loyally serving the King. Hugh had developed over the years a very perceptive mind and was summoned on more than one occasion to England to give King Henry advice about Irish affairs.

In 1230, Hugh de Lacy together with Richard de Burgh were sent by the king to subdue Aedh mac Ruaidri Ó Conchobair, the Irish King of Connacht. Richard de Burgh later became the 1st Baron of Connacht.

Walter de Lacy was a supporter and benefactor to the abbeys of Llanthony and Craswall (Herefordshire), and he also founded the monastery of Beaubec in Ireland. The following year Walter was appointed Castellan and Sheriff of Hereford and appointed custos (Keeper) of the vacant see of Hereford.

Again, Walter de Lacy in 1225 had to raise money to pay fines to the King. By now he had become heavily reliant on loans from European financiers, although this did not stop him from making further substantial donations to religious houses including Llanthony, Prima, and Secunda. He founded the Grand Montine priory at Craswall in Herefordshire. However, his debts finally caught up with him, and on 19th November 1240, the Crown issued orders for the restraint of his estates to recover those debts.

By 1233, William Gorm de Lacy had returned from serving the King in his European struggles. The armies of King Henry III regarded him as the

"chiefest champion in all of Europe".

William Gorm has immediately involved himself once again in Irish affairs. While leading his forces in a skirmish, he was injured and died some days later while sheltering in a house in the Brenie (Breifne) deep in the hills of Northern Ireland. William Gorms wife, Gwenllian, was a younger daughter of Llywelyn the Great, the Prince of Gwynedd, Wales. There is speculation William Gorm, and Gwenllian de Lacy had, at least, two sons, Thomas de Lacy and Henry de Lacy who lived on beyond the fall of the House of de Lacy.

Walter de Lacy's son and heir, Gilbert died before his father in 1234 at Trim Castle and was taken for burial at Llanthony Priory in Monmouthshire England. He had married Isabel Bigod, daughter of Hugh Bigod, 3rd Earl of Norfolk. In 1225 and had two daughters, Margery born in 1228, in Ewyas Lacy, and Maud, who was born in 1230 in Dublin.

Following the death of his estranged first wife. Hugh de Lacy then re-married Emmeline de Riddlesford, the daughter of Walter de Riddlesford about 1242. Hugh de Lacy died one year later in 1243. With still no heir from either marriage. The earldom became extinct, and the Hugh de Lacy estates reverted to the Crown.

Walter died on the 24th February 1241 in Meath, Ireland. He was blind, feeble, bankrupt and without a male heir. A sad ending for a man and a family line that had shaped and ruled both Ewyas Lacy and wider estates in the Welsh Marches, Herefordshire, and Ireland for nearly two centuries.

Because Gilbert had predeceased his father, the de Lacy estates in Normandy, Hertfordshire and

Ireland passed down to his daughters. Margery who died about 1256 and Maud, who died on the 11th of April 1304 in Ireland. Bringing to a sad end, the de Lacy line, founded by Baron Walter de Lacy 1st Lord of Weobley. In the mid 11th century.

The de Lacy family
Grey years.
1241-1641

With the Irish branches of the Baronial de Lacy family now at an end. The best recorded de Lacy history available came to an abrupt halt. But not for, the remaining famous (or infamous) de Lacy Irish family tree who were still to follow in the footsteps of Ilbert and Walter, the sons of Hugh de Lacy of Lassy in Normandy. The first de Lacy's to set foot on English soil way back in 1066. So from where did the remaining de Lacy's descendants come from?

The de Lacy family since 912 AD, had settled in Lassy. Successive generations leading down to Lord Hugh de Lacy, father of Ilbert and Walter. would have uncles and cousins that also carried the name of de Lacy. While they were not found during researching the book, it is unlikely that other de Lacy's of noble birth were not present at the Battle of Hastings. We also know that Hugh, Lord of Meath settled estates on Knights and others close to him. His new powers had enabled Hugh to create Baronetcies without recourse to the King. At least three of the new Barons created were called de Lacy.

A more recorded source of the de Lacy name comes from de Lacy children born out of wedlock. The arranged marriages of the powerful mediaeval aristocracy were not based, on love alone. Marriages were arranged to enhance power, wealth, and landholding. Often these arrangements were loveless the wife's part in the marriage was to produce a male heir to ensure the continued growth of the dynasty. Husbands frequently took a mistress. Where this arrangement blossomed, and children were the outcome. A loving, caring father would provide an estate, and if, in the eyes of the church, he could not legitimise his children, he could at least empower them with his name.

Even from the Baronial family de Lacy, there is the probability of succession in later years. Hugh and Rohese had nine children, four sons, and five daughters: Walter and Hugh (II) then a third son Gilbert de Lacy for whom there are no remaining records of his life. What happened to Gilbert? Did he leave any children?

There is speculation that William Gorm and Gwenllian de Lacy had, at least, two sons, Thomas de Lacy and Henry de Lacy, who lived on beyond their death. In future years, there are many claims of descendants from William Gorm de Lacy.

The name de Lacy, Lacy, Lacey or Lasi is a noble name. Over the centuries, the name Lacy has been feared, hunted, persecuted and respected. From early Tudor times until the eighteenth century to be a Lacy was to mark you as a Catholic and often this was enough to see the establishment of the day intent on persecuting Lacy's along with other Catholics.

And yet families clung to their de Lacy roots.

On a more positive note; Lacy family members tracing their European ancestry and able to determine their European family tree back five or more generations to the mid Nineteenth century. Will probably have a lineage that will stretch back to the eleventh century Lassy in Normandy at the time of Hugh de Lacy.

The Walter de Lacy related branch of the de Lacy family lived, and fought for both their own and Irish causes, for nearly four hundred years without the historical recognition received by the Baronial linage. Ever since and against the King's wishes. Hugh de Lacy married into Irish Royalty,

In 1250, the de Lacy family sponsored Brian O'Neill to be High King of Ireland. Now the de Lacys acted as Irish Chieftains in their opposition to the Anglo-Norman colonials. Yet their colonial past had still not been completely forgotten, now sometimes referred to as 'Sean Gauls' (Old Gauls). The de Lacys were integrating with Irish families and moving ever closer to considering themselves as Irish.

DATELINE November 1272: Following the death of King Henry III King Edward I, (Longshanks) 1272–1307

From this point until the mid-1600's the de Lacy history is even more sparse, this was the 'The grey years' of de Lacy records.

Other Irish branches of the de Lacy name continued after 1250. The name still well known in the east of Ireland, especially in Meath. Of more interest today is an area surrounding Bruree, County Limerick. Here the Christian names of Walter, Hugh and Gilbert continued to be favoured by many of the local de Lacy's. It was reputed that the de Lacy's of County Limerick believed they could trace a direct family line back to William Gorm de Lacy as you will find as you read on.

DATELINE July 1307: the death of King Edward I
King Edward II (Edward of Caernarfon)
7 July 1307 – 25 January 1327

Richard de Burgh, the 2nd Earl of Ulster, was the grandson of Richard de Burgh 1st Lord of Connaught and Egidia de Lacy daughter to Hugh de Lacy 1st Earl of Ulster. In 1308. (a full sixty-five years following the deaths of the original Walter and Hugh) Richard, Earl of Ulster attended the feast of Pentecost at Trim, where he knighted a Walter and Hugh de Lacy to his service. Again History records that Roger Mortimer Earl of March arrived in Ireland in 1308 to enforce his authority. Bringing him into conflict with the de Lacy's, who were trying to increase their estates. During a battle with Richard Clare in 1311. At Bunratty in Thomond. Richard Clare took William de Burgh and Walter de Lacy prisoner. Following a hard-fought battle where many Irish and English fell. There are differing reports whether Walter and Hugh de Lacy were eventually put to death or pardoned.

DATELINE January 1327: Following the death of King Edward II (Edward of Caernarfon) King Edward III, 1327-1377.

In 1348 the 'Black Death' plague struck Ireland via its ports. Carried there by lice or, infected rats in the holds of cargo ships. It spread rapidly through the towns and cities. The Anglo-Irish and their workers were most affected as they all lived in a close community, to each other. By the end of 1348, the plague had spread to Meath, Louth, Kildare and Kilkenny. Colonised Ireland being hit far harder, than Gaelic Ireland, where the population was sparse.

By the second half of the 14th century. Ireland was suffering from in-fighting, the aftermath of the plague, lack of interest by the English throne and a resurgence of power from the Irish chiefs. Lead to a loss of control by the Anglo-Normans, still loyal to the throne, forcing them to retreat to a twenty-mile strip around Dublin. This well-defended area became known as 'The Pale'.

Anglo-Norman families outside of this area were now considered to have gone native and assimilated themselves into the Irish establishment. Now known as 'Old English' by the English, still loyal to the Crown. The de Lacy's formed part of this Irish community.
The de Lacy's now lived beyond the Pale.

DATELINE June 1377:
Following the death of King Edward III
King Richard II
1377 – 1399

Ballingarry Castle, Ballingarry a village in County Limerick, Ireland. Originally a walled mediaeval settlement. A de Lacy family is named there, in records as far back to the early 14th century; The fortified house still referred to as the, de Lacy Castle, situated on Knight Street it was home to the family, who left Ireland as part of the Flight of the Wild Geese in the 1690s.

DATELINE September 1399:
King Henry IV (Bolingbroke) 1399–1413

DATELINE March 1413:
King Henry V (The Star of England) 1413–1422

DATELINE August 1422: King Henry VI
1422 – 1461 and again in 1470 - 1471

In 1460 With the War of the Roses raging in

England. Richard Duke of York had built a power-base in Ireland, left for England leading an Irish army. Among his officers and men was a significant number of Lacy's.

*DATELINE March 1461:
King Edward IV 1471 – 1483
DATELINE April 1483:
King Edward V 1483 – Died same year*

*DATELINE June 1483:
Richard III, 1483 – 1485*

A further mention of the de Lacy's, during this 'grey period' of de Lacy history. In 1483, a Master William de Lacy sent by Richard III of England to Ireland, to negotiate with Gerald FitzGerald, 8th Earl of Kildare better known as the 'Great Earl' Ireland's premier peer. FitzGerald served as Lord Deputy of Ireland from 1477 to 1494; His power had led to him earning the name of 'the uncrowned King of Ireland'. An English de Lacy was again acting as a go-between to the leaders of two countries.

*DATELINE 1485: House of Tudor: Henry VII
1485 -1509*

*DATELINE 1509
King Henry VIII 1509 –1547*

Following the English Reformation, ordered by

Henry VIII in 1530 many English Catholics including some de Lacy families fled to Ireland. It was only within the Dublin Pale that The King's edict was taken up. Most of Ireland resisted and remained steadfastly Catholic.

DATELINE January 1547:
King Edward VI 1547 -1553

DATELINE July 1553:
Queen Mary I (and her husband Phillip) 1553 - 1558

DATELINE November 1558:
Queen Elizabeth I 1558 -1603

Ballingarry Castle at that time was a Geraldine stronghold, held by the locally prominent de Lacy family. In 1569, the castle was captured for Queen Elizabeth I with a death toll of 40 men. The castle changed ownership several times over the ensuing years, and eventually, most of the De Lacy family including John de Lacy settled elsewhere around Ballingarry County, Limerick.

John de Lacy and other local de Lacy family members still rallied to Earl Desmond the head of the Geraldine 'Old English' faction. The de Lacy's were old allies and were eager to support the Desmond rebellion of 1579 against reformation demands made on Ireland by Queen Elizabeth I.

With a pure stroke of irony, Elizabeth sent as her envoy to Earl Desmond, a member of the English de Lacy family, namely Sir John Lacy, to negotiate that Earl Desmond meeting with her demands. Instead, the English John de Lacy found the Earl represented by John de Lacy 'Irishman'. The significant difference, however, was that the Irish John de Lacy would have followed the family faith of that time and been a staunch Catholic. John de Lacy from England was in the Queen's service and would most certainly have been a Protestant. A massive difference in the 1600s. Elizabeth was furious to learn that Earl Desmond was also supported by members of the de Lacy family.

With the talks failing, the Queen sent Sir George Carew, a strict military man to be her president of Southern Ireland. Arriving together with nine thousand English troops. He carried a Queen's writ for the capture dead or alive of Earl Desmond and among others in the Writ the names of fourteen de Lacy's, including John de Lacy.

DATELINE 1603: James I
1603–1625

DATELINE 1625: Charles I 1625-1649

DATELINE 1653:
Lord Protector Oliver Cromwell 1656 – 1658
DATELINE 1658:
Richard Cromwell 1658 - 1659

Lt Colonel Pierce de Lacy
Son of John de Lacy
Later promoted to
General Pierce de Lacy
1619 - 1691

Colonel Pierce de Lacy of the Irish Confederates Army had been engaged in their 1651 revolt against English Rule. Pierce had rushed to Limerick City with his troops to join up with his Senior Officer Owen Roe O'Neill in defence of Limerick. The city was under threat by General Ireton the Son-in-Law of Oliver Cromwell.

On arrival, Colonel de Lacy learned that Owen Roe O'Neill was still fighting elsewhere. He immediately called on the city leaders to uphold the siege until further support arrived. Only to discover that the citizens preferred, and had agreed with General Ireton an honourable surrender. Unable to change the minds of the city leaders. Pierce de Lacy had to yield to their wishes, and he agreed to be one of their emissaries to discuss the terms with the English.

Pierce de Lacy had gained a free pardon for the

majority of the citizens, apart from one thousand soldiers. They were all sentenced to death. To his shock, General Ireton ruled that Colonel de Lacy was also to be among the condemned. Later the sentences were remitted to exile for life. The thousand were put on board a ship to take them into exile in Spain.

on the high seas and well into their journey to Spain, Pierce de Lacy led the prisoners in a mutiny. Overcoming the crew and taking charge of the ship, ordering the Captain to change course for France. Where on arrival Col de Lacy and his new men pledged themselves to the cause of the now exiled King Charles II. Now, under the patronage of King Henry IV of France, they joined up with the Irish Brigade.

DATELINE 1660: Restoration of the English Throne Charles I, 1660-1685

DATELINE 1685:
James II 1685-1688

Following King James II, enthronement in 1685, Pierce de Lacy returned to Ireland. Making an unsuccessful petition, for the restitution of the de Lacy estates. A counterclaim had been made against him. He was facing accusations that he was involved in a plot to annex Ireland from England and re-annex it to France. Thankfully his long service and reputation saved him.

The Flight of the Wild Geese

*Dateline line 1691:
Limerick Ireland*

DATELINE 1688:
Following the death of James II
Queen Mary I, 1688–1694
William III, William of Orange
1688 - 1702

Colonel now
General Pierce de Lacy
1619 - 1691

1689 the Invasion of Ireland by King William III, of Orange. A conflict that would not end until the Battle of the Boyn. 71-year-old General Pierce de Lacy came out of his retirement and volunteered to lead a troop of cavalry under the command of the younger General Patrick Sarsfield, 1st Earl of Lucan, who had control of all Irish forces. To his disgust, he was treated, in a patronising manner by Patrick Sarsfield, who had once been one of his junior subalterns. He dispatched Pierce de Lacy to undertake a minor task.

Ignoring Patrick Sarsfield, Pierce de Lacy left with his loyal soldiers and as many 'irregulars' as he could gather. They marched South to Athlacca where they laid an ambush on an oncoming English regiment whom they defeated. Dispersing the rest who could still run. News of the victory spread rapidly; General de Lacy was back fighting the English. Following this skirmish, his forces rose to five thousand.

Now formed as a guerrilla army known throughout Ireland as the Rapparees, they continued to harass English troops and supply chains. Melting away after each attack to the confusion of their enemies.

King William of Orange had appointed a fellow Dutchman, General Van Ginkel as his military leader in Ireland. With the far more powerful Anglo-Dutch army, Van Ginkel was now marching on Limerick. The city was under the control of Chevalier de Tessé and the Marquis d'Usson, who together commanded the French forces who had sent to aid the Irish.

Even as Van Ginkel's army, was advancing on Limerick. General Pierce de Lacy's army continued to fight a rearguard action slowing their progress. When no longer possible, they turned and rode towards the shelter of the town. The cheers of encouragement from the Irish soldiers on the battlements including the 27 bearing the surname Lacy, turned to cries of rage. A French officer, thinking it was an English charge panicked and ordered "raise the drawbridge" To the horror of the watching Irishmen on the battlements, they saw Pierce de Lacy and his men, many of them kinsfolk, all cut down by the English and Dutch Troops.

General Sarsfield with his now, depleted forces, was still held within the walls of Limerick. He took the command from the two French officers. Sarsfield considered the time was right to accept General van Ginkel's terms of honourable surrender. The conditions had been extended and would include all the besieged soldiers and the citizens of Limerick.

In pardoning the soldiers, Van Ginkel thought he could turn the surrender even more to his advantage. The Dutchman recognised their fighting ability and thought they might be of use to him fighting in Europe under the flag of King William III of England. (William of Orange).

Two Royal standards were raised, just beyond the main gates of Limerick. One placed to the right, flying the English Standard of King William of Orange. To the left was the colours of French King Henry IV. All military forces within the city were now given a stark choice. Stay within the walls and face execution. March out to the English Standard and receive the right to remain in Ireland as part of William of Orange's armed forces. Or march to the left and the colours of King Henry IV, of France and face banishment from Ireland. Fourteen thousand soldiers marched out of the gates. Only 1,044 lined up behind the English banner. The remaining 12,956 including the 27 Lacy's proudly marched to the French flag.

General Van Ginkel was furious; he had underestimated the Irish loathing of the English King. He was, however, a man of honour, he allowed the French officers to commandeer boats to take the Irish soldiers into exile in France. The last of the outstanding de Lacy's who had changed the face of Ireland. We're now leaving Ireland and sowing the seeds of further fame for the family throughout Europe.

Fugitive Irish soldiers had been escaping to France since 1580. Once there, enrolling as mercenary soldiers for any country that would have them. Following the flight of the Irish Earls in 1607, a more formalised group became known as the 'Irish Brigade' made up of the Irish soldiers. This force increased in 1652 with a further thousand Irish prisoners from a British prison ship on the high seas, led by Col Pierce de Lacy in a mutiny to escape Spanish exile and seek sanctuary in France.

Following the fall of Limerick in 1691. The 13,000 defeated, starving soldiers who had opted for exile from Ireland, and deportation to France when they marched out of the gates of Limerick City to choose exile rather than serve under the English flag. The Irish Brigade was now becoming an established division of the French Army. Known throughout Europe as 'The Flight of the Wild Geese'. Many Irishmen were then further recruited, to armies all over Europe.

They included 27 de Lacy kinsman, who had witnessed the death of General de Lacy. Youngest among them was a 13-year-old Peter de Lacy. Ragged, emaciated, barefooted, but head still held high.

"Off you go, boy."

Jeered the onlooking British soldiers

"join the rag bag army of James. What a joke".

They did not know that the boy who they jeered at was to become a Field Marshall that changed the face of Europe.

Count Peter de Lacy
Field Marshall, Supreme Head of the Russian Army. Governor of Livonia. 1678 – 1751
Claimant of direct descent from William Gorm de Lacy

On arrival in France 13-year-old, Peter, his brother and their father, all enrolled in the Irish Brigade. Once rested and back to full strength, they were posted to Brest in 1692. There they received orders to proceed to Nantes and join the French army of Marshal Catinat.

All the Lacy family were engaged in the Nine Year War of 1692 and fought together at the Battle of Marsaglia near Turin in modern day Italy. The battle created a massive number of casualties on both sides. The forces of the Grand Alliance led by Duke Victor Amadeus II of Savoy losing both the action and suffering 10,000 dead, wounded or captured.

Unfortunately, the French casualties included Peter's father and brother who both died taking part in the first formalised bayonet charge.

Following the death of Peter's family, while fighting for Louis XIV in Italy, a 15-year-old Peter was now encouraged by his commander Charles de Croy, to join with him in seeking their fortune elsewhere. Following two years serving in the Austrian army, possibly taking part in the siege of Belgrade, Peter de Lacy followed his commander, into service with the Russian Army.

During the Great Northern War, Tsar Peter the Great, lead a grand alliance of several Countries against the might of the Swedish Army. Despite receiving severe wounds on two separate occasions during the fighting. In 1706, Peter de Lacy rose to the rank of Colonel.

The following year he commanded a brigade at Poltava in central Ukraine, where, with great distinction, Colonel de Lacy helped gain the victory for Russia.

His fame as a soldier grew from this point. With a command as part of Prince Vasily Repnin's army. Peter fought with varying fortune until 1709 when he was given the control as Brigadier-General of the Russian right wing at the battle of Pultava where General Peter de

Lacy put to flight the Swedish Major General Carl Wrangeland and his army. Leading to the total defeat of Charles XII of Sweden.

The Russian success was credited to Peter de Lacy, having put to the Tzar, radical ideas on improving the fighting ability of the Russian soldiers under his command. The Russian troops used to advance as in the past 'sword and shield' days. Line up at a distance, charge and engage. Their muskets often fired as soon as they charged, but they were more often still out of range. Peter de Lacy trained them, among other tactics, to advance as a disciplined unit, discharging their muskets, only on the line officer's order.

The Tzar afterwards complimented Peter de Lacy for detecting these deficiencies and installing a better plan of engagement. Czar Peter acknowledged to de Lacy that his advice was the secret of victory.

His next active service, still under Prince Repnin, was in 1710 at the siege of Riga. Peter de Lacy was the first Russian officer to enter the capital of Livland, and he was appointed the first Russian commander of Riga Castle.

Later in 1721, Peter de Lacy was made Governor of Livonia (parts of modern-day Latvia and Estonia). In 1723 de Lacy on being appointed as a member of the Russian War

Council, contributed his advice on military discipline and training soon after introduced throughout the whole Russian army. Peter de Lacy from having joined the Russian Army as an Irish mercenary recruit had within 28 years risen to reform the entire Russian Army.

On receiving his invitation to the Coronation ceremony of Catherine I, at Moscow in 1724; Peter de Lacy was delighted that he had a place of Honour. In the same year, he celebrated his marriage to the Baltic German, Countess Martha Philippina von Loeser, the widow of the late Count von Funk of Livonia. In 1725, their son Franz Moritz was born in St Petersburg.

Soon after the birth of his son, Peter became General-in-Chief of Infantry and decorated with the Order of St. Alexander Newsky. Dispatched to Poland in October 1733 he entered Warsaw with thirty thousand men, to establish Augustus of Saxony, as the King in opposition to King Stanislaw.
With the defeat of King Stanislaw, to recognise Peter de Lacy's services. King Augustus, presented to him his portrait set in diamonds. Later valued at 25,000 crowns. Along with the portrait, the King also created Peter de Lacy as a Knight of the White Eagle of Poland.

About this time, he was now directed to lead 15,000 troops to the aid of Austria against

France, but peace was declared, in February 1736, and he encamped his army in Bohemia and returned to Vienna. Here he had an interview with the Emperor and Empress where the Emperor awarded Peter de Lacy with the patent of Field Marshal.

In 1736, on his return to Russia, he was sent to take command of the campaign against Turkey. Peter de Lacy at the head of a large army invaded the Crimea and stormed Azov. He routed three thousand Turks, which led to the releasing of innumerable Christian slaves and the capture of much war material. Despite being wounded, during this conflict Peter de Lacy carried on. During the remaining Crimean campaigns that followed, he met with outstanding success and vanquished both. Turk and Tartar. A special medal was created to commemorate his achievements in the Crimea.

In 1741 Peter de Lacy received the supreme Russian command of the war against Sweden, from which he emerged victorious in 1743. Once peace was declared, throughout Russia the news was spread with this message
"It was Marshal de Lacy who taught the Muscovites to beat the King of Sweden and from being the worst in Europe to become the best soldiers in Europe."

In recognition of his services, the Tzarina sent

her private yacht to bring the veteran to Petersburg where he received the thanks of the Royal Court and the acclamation of the people.

Marshal Peter de Lacy then retired from public life and passed his remaining years at his home and estates in Livonia. (A former state which today would have been parts of the states of Latvia and Estonia). Even in retirement, he remained active as the Governor Of Riga. He died at Riga on May 11th, 1751,

His last direction being,
"bury me Christianly and decently without idle pomp".

For a fortnight the bells tolled at intervals while the city and province were in deep mourning for their beloved Governor.

Marshal Franz Moritz Graf von Lacy
Son of Count Peter de Lacy
Count of the Holy Roman Empire St Petersburg
Oct 1725, – till Nov 1801, Vienna

Franz Moritz von Lacy spent his childhood travelling between St Petersburg and the de Lacy home at Riga before leaving in 1737 to be educated for a military career at the newly founded Knight Academy in Legnica, Southern Silesia, in today's Poland. On finishing his education and receiving his commission. Franz Moritz on his father's advice joined the Austrian, not the Russian Army. He joined the forces of his father's old friend Field Marshal Maximilian von Browne; von Browne was also a descendant of the 'Flight of the Wild Geese' his ancestors were also from Limerick and were distant relatives of the de Lacy family.

Between 1745 and 1748 Franz Von Lacy honed his skills as a military leader in Italy, Bohemia, Silesia and the Netherlands all during the War of the Austrian Succession, despite having been wounded twice, by the end of the war become a Lieutenant-Colonel. Then at twenty-five, he became a full colonel and chief of an infantry regiment.

With the outbreak of The Seven-year war in 1756. Colonel Franz Moritz von Lacy was in command of 7,800 regular infantrymen, at the battle that opened the hostilities in the Bohemian city of Lovosice in the present-day Czech Republic, by setting a trap for the oncoming forces of King Frederick of Prussia he could ambush and defeat Frederick's Army putting them to flight.

Despite being injured for the third time, he distinguished himself so much that he received an immediate promotion to Major-General Franz Moritz. Only to be wounded again for the fourth time at the Battle of Prague a year later. He lost his Commander and mentor, Field Marshal von Browne, who was mortally wounded, at the same battle.

In 1757, General Lacy bore a conspicuous role following the great Prussian victory of Breslau and at Leuthen where King Frederick had used his Prussian Army to outflank the Austrians and force a retreat. Despite receiving his fifth wound, General von Lacy and his troops so efficiently covered the retreat of the defeated Austrian Army; they saved the army from collapse. Franz Moritz von Lacy received The Grand Cross of the Order of Maria Theresa for his leadership.
A reformed Austrian Army created a General Staff Council It comprised Field Marshall's Daune, Laudon and newly promoted Lieutenant Field Marshal Lacy. Thus for some years, the actions of Lacy, Daune, and Laudon, is the history of the war with Prussia. Following his role in the battle of Hochkirch (October 15, 1758) Lacy received the Grand Cross of the Order of Maria Theresa.

Upon Empress Maria Theresa placed her son, Prince Joseph II, at the head of Austrian military affairs in 1766, Marshal Franz Moritz von Lacy was made a full Field Marshal and given the role of reforming and administering the Army. He framed new regulations for each arm of the Army and a new code of military law. A vastly improved supply system. As the result of all his work, the Austrian army soldiers increased in numbers, were better equipped, and more cost-effective than it had ever been.

Marshal Franz Moritz von Lacy activities were not only confined to the army. He was in sympathy with Emperor Joseph's innovations seeing him as a prime mover in the scheme of the partition of Poland.

His self-imposed work ethic broke down Lacy's health, and in 1773, he semi-retired to Southern France. Upon Maria Theresa's death, Joseph II became Austrian Emperor. Franz Moritz von Lacy retained the Emperors trust and friendship. He agreed to several more military actions, before retiring to his castle of Neuwaldegg, Vienna. He died there in 1801.

Field Marshall Luis Roberto de Lacy
Born; 1772, San Roque, Nr Cadiz
Died 1817, Palma, Majorca
Posthumously created Duke of Ultonia.

The Spanish assembly or Cádiz Cortes, Had brought into law, the Spanish Constitution of 1812 establishing a constitutional monarchy and removing many of the privileges expected by the ruling aristocracy of Spain.

The Cádiz Cortes refused to acknowledge

Ferdinand until he had sworn to recognise the Spanish Constitution of 1812. King Ferdinand, had other ideas and decided that his power should be absolute. He returned to a population, for whom he had no affection. Helped by a small band of influential nobles, he overthrew the treaty and disbanded the Cádiz Cortes.

Marshal Luis Roberto de Lacy was furious at the outcome arising from the King's return. Many other leading liberal Spanish leaders agreed with him. The war fought to prevent one absolute leader, only to find their King intent on reverting to the same absolute rule.

By 1816 and with Luis once again in Catalonia. He was in touch with his former subordinate General Francis Milans del Bosch. They had both witnessed the injustice and oppression that was sweeping Spain under King Ferdinand's rule. They planned together military and civilian uprising against the monarchy to reinstall the Spanish Constitution of 1812. It was time to act. Luis did not intend to have his revolt fail as so many others had in history. He spent the next six months planning, organising, and inspiring. By April 1817, Luis de Lacy and his supporters were ready to launch their planned revolt later known as the 'Pronouncement of Lacy.'

On the eve of the uprising, while Luis de Lacy

and his aides were making their last-minute preparations, they were stormed by troops, loyal to the King. Someone had betrayed them to the Kings officers. Many of Luis de Lacy's co-conspirators fled leaving him to face arrest. Luis was taken to Barcelona, court-martialed, and sentenced to death on the orders of the King. However, Luis was still regarded as a much-loved wartime hero. His death sentence created a nationwide protest. Fearing an uprising, Luis was taken from the mainland to the island of Mallorca.

Promised a reprieve Luis understood that on arrival he would be pardoned. His quarters were to be at Bellver Castle to await his reprieve. That same night he was led out of his apartment and shot dead against the castle moat wall. Following his long and brilliant career as a soldier, his life ended at the age of 45. Reports said he faced death with 'the same bravery that he had shown in defending his country'.

Following a further three turbulent years of Spanish history. King Ferdinand VII, finally accept the role of a constitutional King. Luis Roberto de Lacy received a posthumous pardon. A public funeral was held to recognise Luis de Lacy as a Spanish war hero. King Ferdinand VII himself, who had three years before ordered Luis's execution, begrudgingly attended the funeral. The King posthumously created Luis as Duke of Ultonia.

Today when the President of Spain faces the Cortes of Madrid, a plaque bearing the name of Luis Roberto de Lacy is among other heroes of Spanish democracy, on the right-hand side of his seat.
Spanish historians and scholars teach that born of a 'distinguished Irish family of the time' No Irish family had achieved greater fame in the military history of Europe than the Lacy family.

There had been a de Lacy presence in Spain since the 1300's During the reign of King John in the 13th century. Many Anglo-Norman lords who had fallen foul of King John fled with their wives to Spain. Including at least one member of the Lacy family was reputed to have married King John's daughter. On reporting back to their Irish relatives that not only was the climate so much better, but Spanish rule was also less turbulent than Ireland under King John. From this small start, a thriving Irish community including many Lacy's assimilated themselves into the Spanish population.

Other notable Spanish de Lacy's that deserve recording. General Peter de Lacy. Peter was the second son of General Piers de Lacy of Limerick and Grandfather to Field Marshall Luis de Lacy. Peter de Lacy had a cousin who was General

Pierce de Lacy-Bellingari. He was part of the de Lacy-Billingari family; the suffix "-Billingari" refers to the de Lacy family originally from Ballingarry, Limerick, also known as "of La Garthe". There was also General Count William de Lacy. Born in Ballyteigue, County Limerick a Grandson of John de Lacy of Bruree. County Limerick

At the time of the Napoleonic wars, within each of the nation's Army, there was thousands of ex-patriot Irish de Lacy's. Most countries had an Irish Brigade of sorts or individuals ready to fight for their adopted home. Either in the Irish Brigades or as individuals. It followed therefore at times; there were de Lacy's on both sides of the battle.

There remained one country the Irish Brigades did not fight for, and that was The British. However, the British Army had many loyal de Lacy's of its own, within all ranks.

By the start of the 18th century, many of the de Lacy families were serving in the armies of the Continent. The de Lacy's had lost most of their estates by default, for making the choice, 'not to join services in the armies of King William I',

Not every branch of the de Lacy family left Ireland with the Wild Geese migration. Patrick De Lacy of Milltown, County Limerick, married

Elizabeth Barry. Their daughter Elizabeth married John Evans. As both John Evans and Elizabeth came from de Lacy stock, tracing back to Gen Pierce de Lacy, they adopted the double-barrelled name of de Lacy Evans. Which became the name of their son, George de Lacy Evans. George was born in 1787 at the family home in Moig, County Limerick. Educated in England at the Royal Military Academy, Woolwich.

General Sir George de Lacy Evans
Soldier, Member of Parliament.
County Limerick, 1787- 1870

George de Lacy Evans started his military career as a cadet with the East India Company. While still in India at eighteen he entered the 22nd (Cheshire) Regiment of Foot. Holding, at first, the junior Officer rank of Ensign, a year later obtaining a full commission as a Lieutenant.

Following the outbreak of the Peninsular war in 1808, George de Lacy Evans transferred to the 3rd Dragoon Guards. He served with them for two years in a staff capacity, where he played both a conspicuous and substantial role, in all the major engagements. Despite receiving a wound at Hormaza during the build-up to the major battle of Vittoria, de Lacy Evans nevertheless insisted on taking part.

While recovering from the injury, he acted in a staff capacity with Sir George Murray. Their mission was to map and illustrate the Pyrenees passes. Back in active service, he twice had his horse shot from under him both at Bayonne and again just as the Peninsular war was ending with the battle of Toulouse.

During the War of 1812, de Lacy Evans was part of the British expeditionary army sent to America. Serving there on the staff of Major General Robert Ross. The Army landed at Benedict on the Maryland Coast. George de Lacy Evans appointment was as deputy quartermaster. An important role for an expeditionary force, thousands of miles away from home.

He was present at the Battle of Bladensburg and soon after, the Burning of Washington. He fought at Baltimore, in September., and in the New Orleans operations in December 1814, on both occasions, he was wounded.

Recognised for his valour and leadership in India, The Peninsular War and the American expedition he was promoted successively, Captain, Major and then Colonel. Three promotions within only six months.

With Napoleon's escape from Elba in February 1815, and was able to quickly take control again of the French government. This lead to the Napoleonic wars reaching a new level. Colonel George de Lacy Evans returned from America, to join Wellington's army in Belgium. To find that he had now been posted to Lieutenant General Sir Thomas Picton's division as deputy quartermaster-general.

General de Lacy Evans was transferred soon after, to the staff of the Duke of Wellington's army. Where he served with distinction at the battle of Quatre Bras, and then again just two days later at the Battle of Waterloo. He remained on the staff of the army of occupation, until its withdrawal in 1818, and then with half-pay, placed on the military reserve.

On his return to Britain, Gen de Lacy Evans was called out to lead the troops, sent to Glasgow during the disturbances of 1819.
He later claimed that he had made numerous unsuccessful requests to serve abroad in the years that followed, letting his resentment to this stagnation of his career, which he attributed to personal malice from the military hierarchy during this low point in his life.

General Sir George de Lacy Evans spirits rouse on receiving from the French Government, The Grand Cross of the French Legion of Honour.
For the next eleven years, Gen George de Lacy Evans spent his enforced early retirement,

pursuing a career as a writer of pamphlets on political matters while trying to secure another military role. His main lines of argument, based on his fear that Russia had designs on taking India from the British. He also campaigned and welcomed the passage of Catholic Emancipation in the Roman Catholic Relief Act of 1829.

His political activities led to him standing for election as the Liberal candidate to Parliament for Rye in East Sussex. He held the seat for two years, but with new boundary changes of 1832, moved and successfully stood for the seat of Westminster, which he held from 1833 to 1841 when he lost, only to win the seat back again in 1846.

During his time in Parliament. George de Lacy campaigned both independently and also with his party on many human matters. He did not find the same parliamentary success, however, that he had achieved in the army.

Life dramatically changed for de Lacy Evans. In 1854 at 66, recalled again to the Army and promoted to Lieutenant General and given command of the 2nd Division under Lord Raglan. His division quickly dispatched to the conflict in Crimea. Their first engagement was at the siege of Sebastopol. Which if taken, would open the port to the allied forces?

Later that year with Sebastopol still in the hands of the Russians. General de Lacy Evans 2nd division took part in the battle of Alma. Working together with other allied forces, they routed the Russians who fell back in disarray to Sebastopol. The British wanted to chase them back to the city which probably would have fallen. The French allies did not agree as they were short on cavalry having relied more on their navy. While Alma was a great victory, a valuable opportunity had been lost.

General de Lacy Evans and his 2nd division next became involved in the battle of Inkerman The Russians tried to make a surprise attack on the 2nd Division. The firing on guard pickets in the valley gave warning to the rest of the Second Division, who rushed to their defensive positions. General De Lacy Evans, the commander of the British Second Division, was severely injured in a fall from his horse. His second in command General Pennefather had to take over temporary and then later full command of the Second Division.

General George de Lacy Evans, who had led his forces with great leadership and bravery, was invalided back home to England. Age and injury had taken its toll on his health, and soon after he died of bronchitis in January 1870.

Trans-Atlantic Geese
James Lacy
1587

James Lacy in 1587 earned his place in the 'de Lacy Chronicles' as the first Lacy to set foot on American soil. He was part of the Raleigh settlement scheme of Virginia.

Unsure of what awaited them beyond the shoreline, they were under orders to make camp and wait for the arrival of the supply ship. Unfortunately, it never turned up, and they all perished. Later talks with the local native tribesmen confirmed they knew the 'new people' were there but had made no contact as they felt no threat to themselves from the 'new people'. So there had been no American establishment of the de Lacy family at that early date.

James Horace Lacy
Plantation Owner. Virginia, USA. Ellwood Plantation, Chatham Manor Plantation 1823-1906

James Lacy, a prosperous businessman and slave owner, lived with his wife Bette at his Ellwood Plantation until the death of Bette's half-sister Hannah Jones Coalter, the widowed owner of Chatham Manor. Arrangements were made by James Lacy, while keeping Ellwood, to buy the more extensive estate, and move his family from Ellwood to Chatham Manor.

Hannah Coalter, following the growing trend towards the emancipation of slaves, had placed within her will, a request that the Chatham Manor slaves, be granted their freedom on her death. The executors of Hannahs last will convinced by James Lacy, that in the matter of the slaves, it must first be put before the courts, to seek legal permission.

James Lacy, a supporter of keeping slaves, learned that his protests had been upheld, by the Virginia court of appeal. The court denied the Chatham slaves the right to freedom, based on the 1857 decision of the American Supreme Court that slaves were property and not persons with a choice.

According to the census of 1860, James Lacy owned 39 slaves at Chatham a further 49 at Ellwood and an additional unknown number, that he rented out to other Virginians. By 1860, almost half a million people, about 31% of the total population of Virginia were slaves.

At the outbreak of the American Civil War in 1861, James Lacy joined the Confederate Army and quickly received the rank of Major working as an aide to General Gustavus W Smith. Major James Lacy was with General Smith at the battle of Seven Pines. Following the hostilities, James was further promoted to transportation inspector in the Mississippi Department.

His brother Rev Beverly Tucker Lacy became Chaplain to General Stonewall Jackson. When General Jackson lost an arm in battle, the Lacy's had it buried at nearby Ellwood. Betty Lacy and the children remained at Chatham Manor until early 1865, only leaving when the estate, was captured by Union troops. All plantation work stopped, and under the new constitution, the slaves were immediately freed.

By the time Chatham Manor was finally restored to James Lacy the building was desolate with much damage both to the house and the grounds. Five thousand panes of window glass smashed, plaster had been broken to reveal bare walls; all the interior carved wood panels were torn off to use as firewood. The house now totally trashed, was uninhabitable.

The lawn had become a graveyard. Without slaves to maintain the plantation and house James Lacy sold Chatham for $23,900 and moved his family back to Ellwood. James Horace Lacy spent the following years, lecturing all over the United States

Captain Patrick DeLacy
Medal of Honor, The Battle of the Wilderness, Virginia May 1864.
(November 25, 1835 – April 27, 1915)

Patrick, born in Carbondale, Pennsylvania

during November 1835. He enlisted as a Unionist soldier: into the 143rd Pennsylvania Infantry where he fought in the American Civil War. Patrick de Lacy received in May 1864 the country's highest award for bravery. The Medal of Honor. Received for running ahead of the line, under concentrated fire, he shot the colour bearer of the Confederate 1st South Carolina Infantry Regiment, thus contributing to the success of the attack.

For this action during the Virginian Battle of the Wilderness, in May 1864. Patrick received a promotion from Private to Sergeant Major, then to Lieutenant before being 'mustered out' of the army Patricks bravery was recognised when he the Medal of Honor in June 1865. He died on 27 April 1915, and his remains interred, at Saint Catherine's Cemetery in Moscow, Pennsylvania. After the war on June 8, 1987, and thanks to the efforts of Elizabeth Hicks Jaquinot, posthumously Patrick was promoted and given the rank of Captain. # During this re-write of de Lacy Chronicles I came across a family website dedicated to Patrick, here is the web address. http://www.patrickdelacy.com

In conclusion

This book, chronicling the onward path of the de Lacy extended family, started in the mid-ninth century. Now ends in the nineteenth century. Over one thousand years of de Lacy history.

We know already that further de Lacy's (or Lacy, Lacey) have left their mark in the twentieth century, but that is another story for another day.

About the creating of this Book

My research started in the usual way, a visit to the library requesting textbooks about the Mediaeval Period in general or the de Lacy Family in particular. Following a frustrating five hours, I emerged with one or two pages of information. Between the exhausting search through the book that the librarian had found for me coupled with the fact that I am dyslexic and hate having to resort to pen and paper, it was clear I would get nowhere by relying on convention.

Rather than give up, after all, I had promised my grandson Louis that I would complete a fact-finding project. Time then to turn to my trusty computer and research online. I had recently at 75 retired, from running my business which had a strong internet presence. I was now on the familiar ground where the facts began to flow.

Names, dates, and incidents now stored in a personal database for further use. At this stage, I realised there was a lot of de Lacy information, and I mean a lot! Not all of it correct either, especially some dissertations and theses that I discovered in PDF files.

Every date I have used I have tried to cross check at least twice. From my mix of information, I found Kings reported to have led armies into battle as young as three years old! Worse still the same mistake would crop up copied into other articles.

No text from other works has been copied into this book, other than, historical names, places, and dates. My whole book has been put through a plagiarism scan and came out at an unavoidable, level of under three percent.

Now, I must pay credit to those sites from which I gained the most support. Where possible, I have shown the website address so you can also explore further if you wish. First, let me acknowledge that without referring to the two major search engines I would still be seeking information to this day.

Google: Finding the most obscure facts with

ease. A date check here a snippet of information there. Where would we be today without Google? So often, taken for granted.
Wikipedia: Once I came to terms with the fact that pieces or pages are submitted by different people, often with their own personal agenda, Wikipedia became my constant companion sitting in an ever-ready open tab at the top of my screen.

De Lacy Books: There have only been two or three books written that cover all or large parts of the de Lacy family history. All appear to be out of print. One survives on the internet but can no longer be downloaded as an e-book. It is, 'The Legacy of the de Lacy, Lacey, Lacy Family.' 1066-1994'. You can still find it in online Google Books. By Gerry Lacey, 1994. https://books.google.com/books?id=rKAKXWXIa9gC If unable to find. Try Google Books and the book title. I kept a download (read-only) copy on my computer and found it useful for cross-reference. The de Lacy legacy gets lost within the close following of history. But if you want to delve deeper into the history of the de Lacy family, I recommend it to you.

The Wikipedia Page De Lacy: Has a vast store of de Lacy information, or you can follow the individual links where available. https://en.wikipedia.org/wiki/De_Lacy

Elizabeth Ashworth Author: My thanks for her guidance on the family of Ilbert de Lacy.
Elizabeth Ashworth has written several novels about members of the de Lacy family. To enable the accuracy of her books Elizabeth has undertaken extensive research on the Ilbert de Lacy family line. This information has been made available to view on her website.
http://elizabethashworth.com/the-de-lacy-family/

Midgley Web Pages: Sound information about The Honour of Pontefract and the de Lacy family at Pontefract. Their website is http://midgleywebpages.com/honour.html.

The History of Ewyas Lacy: History about the Norman Marcher Lords, who settled along the English-Welsh border is limited. This site, however, is packed full with dates places and facts about Walter de Lacy and his descendants. It has proved invaluable in researching the second line of the de Lacy family. http://ewyaslacy.org.uk/doc.php?d=rs_ewy_0201

Foundation for Mediaeval Genealogy: A wealth of information is available here to enable cross-referencing of de Lacy dates, places, and names. Under author's wishes, no text has been transposed into this book. Here is the website should you want to explore.

Mediaeval Lands data content and text are copyright © Charles Cawley, 2006-14.
http://fmg.ac/Projects/MedLands/ENGLISHNOBILITYMEDIEVAL3L-O.htm
On the same site also visit, Ireland then scroll down to Lords of Meath.
http://fmg.ac/Projects/MedLands/IRELAND.htm

wesleyjohnston.com: An easy to read, comprehensive introduction to the de Lacy history in Mediaeval Ireland
http://www.wesleyjohnston.com/users/ireland/past/history/norman_invasion.html.

Navan & District Historical Society: An interesting site for anyone who wishes to know more about Co Meath and the de Lacy Irish years. Visit http://www.navanhistory.ie/
Ballingarry Village: Important information regarding the de Lacy 'Grey Years.'
http://www.ballingarryvillage.com/#!history/c16 1y

My thanks to not only the above sites but the hundreds of others that I have visited over the last three years in the compiling of the de Lacy Chronicles.

Last but certainly not least: I offer my thanks to my wife, Marjorie. I thank her for her patience, encouragement and help in preparing this book.

So what's next?

I have produced for you a low-cost book. A book that would satisfy the curiosity of anybody that would have an interest in the history of the de Lacy family. You will be the judge of my success or not.

There is so much more to tell, to show even? To add full-colour photographs, extend the text to include more about Lacy Castles, etc. Would have more than trebled the cost. I had to add the next steps. My next two projects are now live.

The website. 'www.delacychronicles.com'.
Here I hope together we can indulge in using space and pages more than was possible in this book. Add the colour of pictures of de Lacy castles etc. A platform for Utube videos relating to de Lacy history.

Last but certainly not least! A page dedicated to the de Lacy family tree. Here you can add, or seek, information about your own de Lacy descendants. The site is interactive. Please feel free to use it.

De Lacy Chronicles: The Facebook Page
'de Lacy Chronicles'
A group page dedicated to the history of the amazing de Lacy Barons. The Castles in England and Ireland they built. If your interest is the genealogy of your Lacy name, this site may help. You can find even more Information complete with pictures also to keep you updated about events due to held at de Lacy Castles Pontefract, Clitheroe, Longtown, Ludlow

and Trim in Ireland. You are free to join the site and add your own de Lacy family news!

For more de Lacy information email.
delacychronicles@gmail.com

Printed in Great Britain
by Amazon